TWELFTH NIGHT

Translated

William Shakespeare

translated by

SJ Hills

Faithfully Translated
into Performable Modern English
Side by Side with Original Text

Includes Stage Directions

TWELFTH NIGHT,
or What You Will

Book 27 in a series of 42

This Work First Published In 2023
by DTC Publishing, London.
www.InteractiveShakespeare.com

This paperback edition first published in 2023

Typeset by DTC Publishing.

Translated by SJ Hills from
Twelfth Night, Or What You Will
by Shakespeare, circa 1601.
Additional material by SJ Hills

First Edition. A-9b-7x10

ISBN 979-8-859-81425-1

Interactive Shakespeare
Making the past accessible

SJ Hills Writing Credits: Dramatic Works.

Shakespeare Translated Series. Modern English With Original Text.
Faithfully translated line by line for students, actors and fans of Shakespeare.

Macbeth Translated
Romeo & Juliet Translated
Hamlet Translated
A Midsummer Night's Dream Translated
Othello Translated
Twelfth Night Translated
Macbeth For All Ages

Dramatised Classic Works.
Twenty-two dramatised works written and produced by SJ Hills for Encyclopaedia Britannica, based on classic stories including Shakespeare, for audiences of all ages around the world.

Greatest Tales of the World. *Vol 1.*
Greatest Tales of the World. *Vol 2.*

New Works Inspired By Classic Restoration Comedy Plays.

Scarborough Fair - inspired by *The Relapse*
To Take A Wife - inspired by *The Country Wife*
Wishing Well - inspired by *Epsom Wells*
Love In A Nunnery - inspired by *The Assignation.*

Modernised English Classic Works.

The Faerie Queene
Beowulf

Dedicated to my four little terrors;
Melody
Eve
James
Hamilton

With my grateful thanks to John Hills without whose patronage this work and other works in the series would not have been possible.

"*From an ardent love of literature, a profound admiration of the men who have left us legacies of thought and beauty, and, I suppose, from that feature in man that induces us to strive to follow those we most admire, and looking upon the pursuit of literature as one of the noblest in which no labour should be deemed too great, I have sought to add a few thoughts to the store already bequeathed to the world. If they are approved, I shall have gained my desire; if not, I shall hope to receive any hints in the spirit of one who loves his work and desires to progress.*"

R. Hilton. 1869

PREFACE

When we studied Shakespeare at school we had to flick back and forth to the notes at the back of the book to understand a confusing line, words we were not familiar with, expressions lost in time, or even current or political references of Shakespeare's time.

What if the text was rewritten to make each line clear without looking up anything?

There are plenty of modern translations just for this. But they are cumbersome to read, no flow, matter of fact translations (and most this author has found are of varying inaccuracy, despite being approved by exam boards).

As a writer and producer of drama, I wanted not only to translate the play faithfully line by line, but also to include the innuendos, the political satire, the puns and the bawdy humour in a way which would flow and bring the work to life for students, actors prepping for a performance or lovers of the work to enjoy today, faithful to the feel and meaning of the original script and language without going into lengthy explanations for a modern day audience.

A faithful line-by-line translation into modern phrasing that flows, along with additional staging directions making the play interesting to read, easy to understand, and very importantly, an invaluable study aid.

For me it all started at about eight or nine years of age. I was reading a comic which contained the story of Macbeth serialized in simple comic strip form. I could not wait to see what happened next so I rushed out to the public library to get a copy of the book. Of course, when I got it home I didn't even recognise it as being the same story. It made no sense to me, being written in 'Olde English' and often using 'flowery' language. I remember thinking at the time that one day I should write my version of the story for others to understand.

Years went by and I had pretty much forgotten my idea. Then quite by chance I was approached by Encyclopaedia Britannica to produce a series of dramatised classic dramas as educational aids for children learning English as a second language. Included in the selection was Romeo And Juliet which I was to condense down to fifty minutes using modern English.

This brought flooding back the memories of being eight years old again, reading my comic and planning my modern version of Shakespeare. In turn it also led me to the realisation that even if a reader could understand English well, this did not mean they could fully understand and enjoy Shakespeare. I could understand English, yet I did not fully understand some of Shakespeare's text without serious research. So what hope did a person whose first language was not English have?

After some investigation, I discovered there was a great desire around the world to understand the text fully without the inconvenience of referring to footnotes or side-lines, or worse still, the internet. How can one enjoy the wonderful drama with constant interruption? I was also surprised to discover the desire was equally as great in English speaking countries as ones whose first language was not English.

The final kick to get me started was meeting fans of Shakespeare's works who knew scripts off by heart but secretly admitted to me that they did have trouble fully understanding the meaning of some lines. Although they knew the storyline well they could miss some of the subtlety and innuendo Shakespeare was renowned for. It is hardly surprising in this day and age as many of the influences, trends, rumours, beliefs and current affairs of Shakespeare's time are not valid today.

I do not pretend my work is any match for the great master, but I do believe in the greater enjoyment for all. These great works deserve to be understood by all, Shakespeare himself wrote for all levels of audience, he would even aim his work to suit a particular audience at times – for example changing historical facts if he knew a member of royalty would be seeing his play and it would cause them any embarrassment, or of course to curry favour with a monarch by the use of flattery.

I have been as faithful as possible with my version, but the original, iambic pentameter, (the tempo and pace the lines were written for), and other Elizabethan tricks of the trade that Shakespeare was so brilliant at are not included unless vital to the text and meaning. For example, rhyming couplets to signify the end of a scene, for in Shakespeare's day there were no curtains, no lights and mostly static scenery, so scene changes were not so obvious, these couplets, though not strictly necessary, are included to maintain the feel of the original.

This makes for a play that sounds fresh to today's listening audience. It is also a valuable educational tool; English Literature courses often include a section on translating Shakespeare. I am often asked the meaning of a particular line, sometimes scholars argue over the meaning of particular lines. I have taken the most widely agreed version and the one which flows best with the story line where there is dispute, and if you read this translation before reading the original work or going to see a stage version, you will find the play takes on a whole new meaning, making it infinitely more enjoyable.

SJ Hills. London. 2018

AUTHOR'S NOTE

This version contains stage directions. These are included purely as a guide to help understand the script better. Any director staging the play would have their own interpretation of the play and decide their own directions. These directions are my own personal interpretation and not those of Shakespeare. You may change these directions to your own choosing or ignore them completely. For exam purposes these should be only regarded as guidance to the dialogue and for accuracy should not be quoted in any studies or examinations.

Current published editions are a mix of the early published editions. Although modern editions largely agree there will be some differences between current versions, so line numbers between two different editions of Twelfth Night will not match. For this reason there are no line numbers included in this edition.

To aid in understanding speeches and for learning lines, where possible, speeches by any character are not broken over two pages unless they have a natural break. As a result of this, gaps will be noticeable at the bottom of pages where the next speech will not fully fit onto the page. This was intentional. A speech cannot be fully appreciated if one has to turn the page back and forth when studying or learning lines.

Shakespeare's use of pre-existing material was not considered a lack of originality. In Elizabethan times copyright law did not exist, copying whole passages of text was frequently practiced and not considered theft as it is today. Nowadays, stage and movie productions are frequently 'adaptations' from other sources, the only difference being the need to obtain permission or rights to do so, unless the work is out of copyright.

The real skill Shakespeare displays is in how he adapts his sources in new ways, displaying a remarkable understanding of human psyche and emotion, and including a talent at building characters, adding characters for effect, dramatic pacing, tension building, interspersed by short bouts of relief before building the tension even further, and above all of course, his extraordinary ability to use and miss-use language to his and dramatic, bawdy or playful advantage.

It has been said Shakespeare almost wrote screenplays, predating modern cinema by over 400 years, however you view it, he wrote a powerful story and understood how to play on human emotions and weaknesses.

This play was written during the reign of Queen Elizabeth I. As Shakespeare often referred to the reigning monarch in his plays indirectly and often performed his plays before the monarch this is useful to know.

HISTORIC NOTES

Shakespeare's *Twelfth Night* is set in Illyria which was an area in antiquity made up of united prefectures (regions) each ruled by a prefect. It was situated on the opposite side of the Adriatic sea to Italy in the region now referred to as The Balkans. It has a remarkably complex history of invasions and boundary changes and even in Shakespeare's time was no longer known as Illyria, which had by then become a mythical 'country' from the public perspective, and is probably why Shakespeare chose it; the public could view it as an exotic far-flung land where everything was very different from life in England.

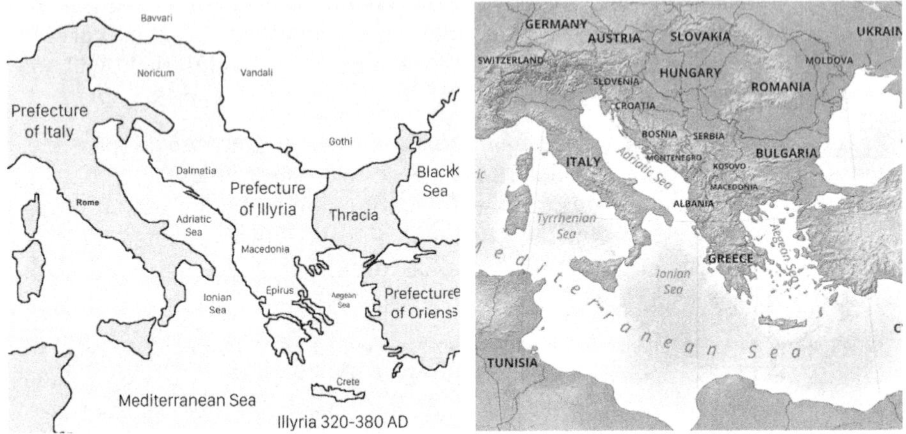

Illyria in antiquity

Modern day Balkans

Twelfth Night, or What You Will is a romantic comedy by William Shakespeare, believed to have been written around 1601–1602 as entertainment for the close of the Christmas season and first performed on the Twelfth Night in 1602 before Elizabeth I, Queen of England.

It was an immediate success and is still performed regularly. While it is a light-hearted play involving mistaken identity, love triangles, and comedic characters, it also has a serious side, exploring themes of identity, gender, love and greed.

The play is believed to be based on two Italian sources: the story of Viola and Sebastian from Matteo Bandello's *Novelle* (1565) and the story of the Countess Olivia from *Il Pecorone* (1565) by Giovanni Fiorentino. Other lesser sources, include Plautus's *Menaechmi* and Terence's *Andria*. However, Shakespeare took these sources and transformed them into something new and original, something he was a master of.

Twelfth Night reflects the religious tensions of the time, England was a Protestant country, Catholicism – the practice of which carried severe penalties, including death – was banned, and the Puritans, who were extremely anti-Catholicism, were rising in popularity, though they were not to everyone's taste. Shakespeare makes some derogatory references to their pious behaviour and their bigotry, suggesting he was not in favour of them. The play also reflects the social and political standings of England at the time.

It is suggested that Shakespeare was a Catholic sympathiser, we know his father was loosely connected with the Catholic Gunpowder Plot to blow up parliament along with King James in 1605 which would occur three years after this play was first performed, and it is possible that Shakespeare based so many plays in Italy, not only because it was considered an exotic location, but also because it was the most Catholic country in Europe, so mentioning Catholic practises could be excused.

The play's title refers to the twelfth night after Christmas, the date of the Christian religious ceremony of Epiphany, which in Shakespeare's time was a time of feasting and merrymaking, and his play, *Twelfth Night,* is generally assumed to have been performed as festive entertainment before the Queen on this actual day - or was it.

For here lies the complication. We have to remember that in Shakespeare's lifetime, on the order of Pope Gregory XIII, the calendar was changed to overcome the slight inaccuracies of the previous Julian calendar.

Although the church in Europe had adopted the new calendar, Queen Elizabeth, who was head of the Church of England (after her father Henry VIII had done a middle-ages Brexit and split from the Catholic church) resisted the change, causing much confusion in England. People had to carry an almanac with both calendars printed side by side.

The Twelfth Night was celebrated on January 6th, a day when people sang songs, made merry drinking alcohol, danced, and ate '*Twelfth Night Cake*' in which a pea and a bean were hidden. The man who discovered the bean would be proclaimed Lord or King of Misrule for the day, while the lady who found the pea would be Lady or Queen of Misrule. The Lord of Misrule was usually a servant who then led the drinking and debauchery, as Twelfth Night was traditionally a day where servants were allowed to swap roles with their masters.

Within the play, Feste the Fool, Sir Toby Belch, and Sir Andrew Aguecheek can all be considered versions of the Lord of Misrule, with Maria being the Lady of Misrule. Feste's song at the end of the play suggests the festivities are over and debauchery is once again frowned upon.

THE CALENDARS.

The Gregorian Calendar was introduced in October 1582, twenty years before this play was first performed, but Elizabeth I resisted this change. As a result future scholars studying Shakespeare failed to notice that Sunday 27 December 1601 in the old Julian calendar was, according to the new Gregorian calendar, Sunday 6 January 1602, the date of the Twelfth Night.

We know from records that the performance before the queen on 6th Jan 1602 was not by Shakespeare's company – but they did perform on December 27th 1601 – so it was possibly recorded using the old calendar date, the one Elizabeth I recognised.

This also partly explains the tag line to the play – "Or As You Wish". It was Elizabeth's wish that the calendar remained as it was, and what the queen said everyone obeyed, if she wished to celebrate Twelfth Night on the old date, so be it.

This is unimportant to the plot but explains the confusion about dates and performances.

Twelfth Night was the religious festival of Epiphany which falls twelve days after Christmas Day and marks the end of Christmas celebrations. You can imagine the confusion of the change of date in the days when there was no mass communication among the general public, a lot of whom were illiterate. People carried almanacs - printed sheets showing moon phases, notable religious dates and the two calendars side by side.

Old Julian Date		New Gregorian Date		
Dec 24th	Fasting	Jan 3rd		
Dec 25th	Christmas Day	Jan 4th	New Moon	
Dec 26th	Feast of Steven the martyr	Jan 5th		
Dec 27th	John Evangelist day	Jan 6th	Epiphany	
Dec 28th	Innocents day	Jan 7th		

A reproduction of an almanac showing both calendars side by side.

Anagrams.

In the play Shakespeare uses anagrams, a popular craze of the time, and it is known that Elizabeth I was a big fan of them.

They are explained as they appear in the text, but it should be known that this has led to confusion through the centuries, and has only recently been adopted as the meaning behind confusing words such as the unknown philosopher '*Quinopolus*'.

M.O.A.I.

Again, scholars have argued what M.O.A.I. could mean for centuries. We now know that it referred to an incident before Queen Elizabeth I where a nobleman, outrageously dressed, kissed the Queen's hand. This gentleman was a source for the character of Malvolio and his outrageous yellow tights and cross-garters.

This is all explained in the text at the relevant point. Elizabeth I would have recognised the meaning behind this – a private joke between Shakespeare and Elizabeth and her close social circle.

Order Of Scenes.

Originally, the second scene of the play was performed as the opening scene, and this makes a lot of sense. The play here is written in the order established today, beginning with the famous opening line "If music be the food of love…", but that's not the way it would have started when performed to Elizabeth I.

If you would like to experience the play as originally performed, start from Act I, Scene II (page 19), and jump back to Scene I (page 16) when it ends. Then skip forward to Scene III (page 23).

"What You Will"

'*What you will*' had two meanings, one being the expression meaning 'whatever you like' or 'do what you want to do', or simply in modern language 'whatever'. The other being for the benefit of Queen Elizabeth I, 'what you wish/desire/order'.

As stated earlier, the queen's version of which calendar to use and therefore which date to celebrate Twelfth Night was entirely up to her, regardless of and in defiance with the head of the Catholic church, the Pope. The queen would have recognised the significance of this title and probably have been flattered.

Asides.

Actors of this play often involve the audience by speaking their asides (thoughts) directly to the audience, sometimes for comedic effect. While it is unusual to 'break the fourth wall' in drama, *Twelfth Night* is a comedy not meant to be taken seriously, and in comedy this can be acceptable.

A comedy in Elizabethan times meant a light-hearted play with a happy ending. What we call comedians today, they called clowns.

Twins.

Finally, the inclusion of twins coming back from the dead and being re-united. There are personal implications here, Shakespeare had lost his son Hamnet, but Hamnet's twin sister had survived. We know through his writing that this affected Shakespeare deeply, Hamnet was his only son, and he dreamed of Hamnet being re-united with his twin sister.

Trivia.

The two lead female characters' names are anagrams of each other under Elizabethan rules – Olivia and Viola.

Identical twins are only ever the same sex, but since females could not act in Shakespeare's time male twins could play the two parts convincingly.

DRAMATIS PERSONAE

DUKE ORSINO,	Duke of Illyria.
VALENTINE,	} Gentlemen attending the Duke.
CURIO,	}
OLIVIA,	A Wealthy Countess.
SIR TOBY BELCH,	Uncle to Olivia.
SIR ANDREW AGUECHEEK,	Friend to Sir Toby.
MALVOLIO,	Steward to Olivia.
MARIA,	Maid to Olivia.
FABIAN,	Servant to Olivia.
FESTE THE CLOWN,	Jester to Olivia.
VIOLA,	Shipwrecked twin sister to Sebastian, sometimes disguised as a man named Cesario.
A CAPTAIN,	Friend to Viola.
SEBASTIAN,	Shipwrecked twin brother to Viola.
ANTONIO,	A Sea Captain, friend to Sebastian.

1st Officer, 2nd Officer, Lords, Priest, Sailors,
Musicians, Servants and other Attendants.

CONTENTS

Scene.
A city in Illyria,
and a seacoast near it.
16th Century.

ACT I

ILLYRIA

WHERE OUR PLAY IS SET

"IF MUSIC BE THE FOOD OF LOVE PLAY ON"

ACT I

ACT I SCENE I

The Palace Of Duke Orsino In Illyria.

Note: Duke Orsino is deeply infatuated with the absent, wealthy countess, Olivia. Musicians are playing romantic music which makes Orsino feel even more love-sick. As the music is making his feelings of love painfully swell, feeding his love, he asks the musicians to play more so he'll have so much of the "food of love" his desire for the music will be overwhelmed and he'll sicken of it, he hopes it will have the same effect on his feelings of love.

To show characters are comedic or to vary the overall structure of the play, Shakespeare sometimes writes lines in prose rather than the usual blank verse (a form of poetry which doesn't rhyme except for dramatic effect). He moves between prose and verse to give his characters depth and variety by breaking the rhythm. Deliberate bawdy use of words is underlined, rhymed lines are in italics.

NB: If you are reading this play in its original scene order, start at Scene II, page 19. (see Historic Notes at start of book, page 10).

Musicians play music before a gloomy looking Duke Orsino, Curio his personal attendant, and various other lords.

As a song ends, Duke Orsino gestures the musicians to continue playing, he pines for his unrequited love, the wealthy Countess Olivia, opening the play with one of Shakespeare's famous lines.

DUKE ORSINO

(*to musicians*) If music makes love grow fonder, then play on. Give me such excess of it that my fondness sickens and dies.

DUKE ORSINO

If music be the food of love, play on,
Give me excess of it, that, surfeiting,
The appetite may sicken and so die.

The band play again.

DUKE ORSINO (CONT'D)

(*to self, groaning*) Oh, that passage of music again! It has such a sad final cadence. Oh, to my ear it was the sweet sound of the wind as it breathes upon a bank of violets, stealing their scent and bringing a new one to them.

DUKE ORSINO

That strain again! - it had a dying fall.
O, it came o'er my ear like the sweet sound
That breathes upon a bank of violets,
Stealing and giving odour.

He continues listening to the music in angst.

He then decides the music is no longer having the desired effect.

DUKE ORSINO (CONT'D)
(*ordering the band*) Enough, no more. It's no longer so sweet sounding.

DUKE ORSINO
Enough, no more;
'Tis not so sweet now as it was before.

THE BAND STOP PLAYING

DUKE ORSINO (CONT'D)
(*to self, sighing*) Oh, spirit of love, how strong and insatiable you are! As hungry as the sea, and as large an appetite. But nothing that love consumes, however perfect, lasts. It quickly loses its value, diminishing by the minute. Love is as changeable as the wind and takes on as many forms.

DUKE ORSINO
O spirit of love, how quick and fresh art thou
That, notwithstanding thy capacity
Receiveth as the sea, nought enters there
Of what validity and pitch* soe'er
But falls into abatement and low price
Even in a minute. So full of shapes is fancy
That it alone is high fantastical.

**Note: 'Pitch' – height. A falconry term meaning the bird's highest point of flight. Shakespeare used falconry terms often in his writings, a subject he was very familiar with.*

CURIO
Will you go hunting, my lord?

DUKE ORSINO
For what, Curio?

CURIO
The hart.

DUKE ORSINO
I do already.

CURIO
Will you go hunt, my lord?

DUKE ORSINO
What, Curio?

CURIO
The hart.

DUKE ORSINO
Why, so I do,

HE PLACES HIS HAND UPON HIS HEART.

DUKE ORSINO (CONT'D)
The dearest part of me. Oh, when I first laid eyes on Olivia I thought she cleansed the air of all ills. That instant I was turned into a hart, and my desires, like savage, cruel hounds, have pursued me ever since.

DUKE ORSINO
the noblest that I have.
O, when mine eyes did see Olivia first
Methought she purged the air of pestilence.
That instant was I turned into a hart,
And my desires, like fell* and cruel hounds,
E'er since pursue me.*

**Note: 'Fell' – terrible ferocity. A meaning not in common use today. The saying 'One fell swoop' (originally from Macbeth, see Macbeth Translated by SJ Hills for further information) which then described a bird of prey attacking all the young in a nest in one savage swoop down from the sky, now has the meaning of 'everything at once, all in one go'. The word 'felon' derives from the original meaning.*

'Cruel hounds pursue me' – from Ovid's 'Metamorphoses'. Actaeon is transformed into a hart (stag) by the goddess Diana after he sees her bathing naked and falls in love with her. He is then pursued and savagely torn apart by his own dogs.

ENTER VALENTINE ANOTHER ATTENDANT TO THE DUKE.

DUKE ORSINO (CONT'D) Well then? What news from her?	DUKE ORSINO How now, what news from her?

VALENTINE ANSWERS AS IF IT IS NOT THE FIRST TIME HE'S BEEN UNSUCCESSFUL IN MEETING THE DUKE'S LOVE INTEREST, OLIVIA.

VALENTINE SPEAKS PRETENTIOUSLY.

VALENTINE If it so pleases my lord, I was again refused admittance. But her maid did give me this answer for you – her lady's face shall not be revealed to the sky for seven summers, like a nun she'll be veiled while out walking, and will water her chamber with tears every day to preserve in salty water the love she held for her dead brother. She wishes to keep her sad memories alive and fresh.	VALENTINE So please my lord, I might not be admitted; But from her handmaid do return this answer: The element itself, till seven years' heat, Shall not behold her face at ample view; But like a cloistress she will veiled walk, And water once a day her chamber round With eye-offending brine: all this to season A brother's dead love, which she would keep fresh And lasting in her sad remembrance.
DUKE ORSINO Oh, she owns such a sensitive, tender heart in that fine body, but uses it all up on the love of a mere brother. How can she love when Cupid's rich golden arrow has killed all other affections that live within her. When she is once again filled with love, desire and emotion, she will find the sweet perfection of passion ruling over her. *Lead me away to sweet beds of flowers.* *Where love's thoughts lie rich and pass by the hours.*	DUKE ORSINO O, she that hath a heart of that fine frame To pay this debt of love but to a brother, How will she love when the rich golden shaft* Hath killed the flock of all affections else That live in her; when liver, brain, and heart,* These sovereign thrones*, are all supplied and filled, Her sweet perfections, with one self king! *Away before me to sweet beds of flowers;* *Love-thoughts lie rich when canopied with bowers.*

**Note: 'Golden shaft' – Cupid's arrow. A gold tipped arrow made a person fall in love, a lead tipped arrow had the opposite effect.*

The liver, brain, and heart are the 'sovereign thrones' which control the three attributes of love. The liver is the throne of desire, the brain is the throne of reasoning, and the heart is the throne of emotion. Orsino means that when Olivia finally falls in love she will be complete. "A woman receiveth completion by the man [through marriage]" said Aristotle.

NB: If you are reading this play in the original scene order, now jump forward to page 23.

ACT I SCENE II

A SEA COAST OF ILLYRIA.

Note: Illyria was an area in antiquity situated on the opposite side of the Adriatic sea to Italy in the region now referred to as The Balkans. In Shakespeare's time Illyria no longer existed, which is probably why Shakespeare chose it; the public could view it as an exotic far-flung land where everything was very different from life in England.

Important Note: This scene was originally the opening scene, and this makes a lot of sense. The famous opening line "If music be the food of love..." was not the way it started when performed to Elizabeth I in 1601 or 1602, depending on whether you use the Julian or Gregorian calendar. (see historic notes at front of book).

NB: If you wish to experience the play as originally performed, start here from Act I Scene II and jump back to Scene I (page 16) when it ends. Then skip forward to Scene III (page 23).

A SMALL BOAT CONTAINING VIOLA (A YOUNG WOMAN), A SEA CAPTAIN, AND SOME SAILORS COMES ASHORE ON THE COASTLINE OF A WARM EXOTIC COUNTRY.

THEY WALK UP THE SHORE, WET AND EXHAUSTED.

VIOLA
Friends, what country is this?

VIOLA
What country, friends, is this?

CAPTAIN
This is Illyria, my lady.

CAPTAIN
This is Illyria, lady.

VIOLA
(*upset*) What am I doing in Illyria? My brother is in heaven.
(*she pauses, weighing things up in her mind*) Perhaps with any luck he didn't drown - what do you think, sailors?

VIOLA
And what should I do in Illyria?
My brother he is in Elysium.*
Perchance* he is not drowned - what think you,
sailors?

**Note: 'Elysium' – In Greek mythology, the place at the ends of the earth to which heroes were taken by the gods after death. The classical version of heaven.*

'Perchance' – used in wordplay four times in as many lines with different meanings. The translation uses the word 'luck' to retain the word play.

1. 'Perchance' – Perhaps.
2. 'Perchance' – By chance.
3. 'Perchance' – Perhaps and by chance.
4. 'Chance' – Luck.

CAPTAIN
It was with luck that you yourself were saved.

CAPTAIN
It is perchance* that you yourself were saved.

VIOLA
(*upset*) Oh, my poor brother!
(*pulling herself together*) So by that same luck he may also be saved.

VIOLA
O my poor brother! - and so perchance* may he be.

CAPTAIN
True, madam, and to comfort you with further tales of luck, I can assure you that after our ship was wrecked, when you and the few saved with you clung to our drifting lifeboat, I saw your brother, wisely in such perilous circumstances, tying himself to a strong ship's mast floating in the sea – courage and the will to survive guiding him – and like Arion, who was saved by riding on a dolphin's back, I saw him riding the waves until he disappeared from sight.

CAPTAIN
True, madam; and, to comfort you with chance*,
Assure yourself, after our ship did split,
When you and those poor number saved with you
Hung on our driving boat, I saw your brother,
Most provident in peril, bind himself
- Courage and hope both teaching him the practice -
To a strong mast that lived* upon the sea;
Where, like Arion* on the dolphin's back,
I saw him hold acquaintance with the waves
So long as I could see.

**Note: 'Lived' – floating. A nautical term for a buoyant ship or object. There is a number of nautical terms used throughout the play.*

Arion, c. 700 BC, was an ancient Greek poet credited with inventing the dithyramb (a circular chorus). Apart from his musical inventions, Arion is famed for the myth of being captured by pirates and miraculously rescued by dolphins, Not to be confused with the Arion of Greek mythology, a divinely-bred, black-maned horse that Heracles rode into battle and which later saved the life of Adrastus when all other leaders were killed.

VIOLA, MORE HOPEFUL NOW, HANDS THE CAPTAIN A GOLD COIN.

VIOLA
For telling me this, here's a gold coin. My own escape gives me hope, and your words serve to strengthen the likelihood of a similar outcome for him.

VIOLA
For saying so, there's gold.*
Mine own escape unfoldeth to my hope,
Whereto thy speech serves for authority,
The like of him.

**Note: 'Gold' – a valuable coin or jewellery. To give silver would be less valuable.*

VIOLA LOOKS ABOUT HER AT THE UNFAMILIAR LANDSCAPE.

VIOLA (CONT'D)
Do you know this country?

VIOLA
Know'st thou this country?

CAPTAIN
Aye, madam, I know it well. I was born and bred less than three hours journey from this very spot.

CAPTAIN
Ay*, madam, well, for I was bred and born
Not three hours' travel from this very place.

**Note: 'Ay' – Yes. Old spelling of aye, and a nautical word for 'yes'. Aye, aye, captain.*

VIOLA Who rules this place?	VIOLA Who governs here?
CAPTAIN A noble duke, both in name and by nature.	CAPTAIN A noble duke, in nature as in name.
VIOLA What is his name?	VIOLA What is his name?
CAPTAIN Orsino.	CAPTAIN Orsino.
VIOLA Orsino? I have heard my father mention him. He was unmarried then.	VIOLA Orsino! I have heard my father name him. He was a bachelor then.
CAPTAIN And he is now, or he was very recently. About a month ago when I left from here there were fresh rumours – you know how commoners gossip about the ruling classes – that he pursued the love of the beautiful Olivia.	CAPTAIN And so is now, or was so very late; For but a month ago I went from hence, And then 'twas fresh in murmur -as, you know, What great ones do, the less will prattle of *- That he did seek the love of fair Olivia.

**Note: 'What great ones do, the less will prattle of' – commoners gossiping about the upper classes. This was for the benefit (and egos) of the upper classes and royalty who would come to see the play and would have raised a laugh among them.*

VIOLA Who's she?	VIOLA What's she?
CAPTAIN A chaste maiden, the daughter of a count who died some twelve months ago leaving her under the protection of his son, her brother. But he also died shortly after his father. Her dear love for him, so they say, causes her to shun the company and sight of all men.	CAPTAIN A virtuous maid*, the daughter of a count That died some twelvemonth since, then leaving her In the protection of his son, her brother, Who shortly also died; for whose dear love, They say, she hath abjured the company And sight of men.

**Note: 'Virtuous maid' - unmarried and still a virgin. Viola has a lot to sympathise with Olivia, being unmarried and having possibly lost her own brother.*

Viola's age is never revealed but it is generally assumed to be in her early twenties.

VIOLA Oh, I wish I served that lady, and might be kept hidden from the world till I had put my mind to rest by knowing the position of my own inheritance.	VIOLA O that I served that lady, And might not be delivered to the world, Till I had made mine own occasion mellow, What my estate* is.

**Note: 'Estate' – property, which she will inherit if her brother is no longer living.*

CAPTAIN
That will be hard to achieve, as she will not allow any visits, none at all, not even the Duke's.

CAPTAIN
That were hard to compass,
Because she will admit no kind of suit*,
No, not the duke's.

**Note: 'Suit' – having the double meaning of making a request of someone or pursuing them romantically.*

VIOLA
There is a good nature in you, captain, and though a kind exterior often hides a malicious interior, I do believe you have a mind that matches your good, outward appearance. I implore you – and I'll pay you handsomely – conceal my identity, help me disguise myself in whatever way necessary to achieve my aims. I wish to serve this duke. You shall introduce me to him as a eunuch. It will be worth your while as I can sing and perform for him in many musical ways which will make me invaluable to his service.
Whatever else happens, plans I will make
Just keep them silent for both of our sake.

VIOLA
There is a fair behaviour in thee, captain,
And though that nature with a beauteous wall
Doth oft close in pollution, yet of thee
I will believe thou hast a mind that suits
With this thy fair and outward character.
I prithee - and I'll pay thee bounteously -
Conceal me what I am, and be my aid
For such disguise as haply shall become
The form of my intent. I'll serve this duke:
Thou shalt present me as an eunuch* to him.
It may be worth thy pains, for I can sing
And speak to him in many sorts of music
That will allow me very worth his service.
What else may hap to time I will commit;
*Only shape thou thy silence to my wit.**

**Note: Viola will not sing for Orsino, instead she becomes a page to him.*

CAPTAIN
I'll be your mute, if his eunuch you'll be,
And if my tongue blabs, take my eyes from me.

CAPTAIN
Be you his eunuch, and your mute* I'll be;*
*When my tongue blabs, then let mine eyes not see.**

**Note: 'Eunuch' – men castrated when they were young to keep their voice high for singing, and also attendants in Turkish harems where they could be trusted as they had no desire for the many wives of a sultan.*

'Mutes' were dumb servants who also served with Eunuchs in the Harem. Although mute now means unable to speak, then it meant a deaf person, and as a deaf person cannot hear speech they could not overhear any secrets. In the theatre world, a 'mute' has no speaking parts.

VIOLA
Thank you. Now, lead the way.

VIOLA
I thank thee. Lead me on.

**Important Note: The rhyming couplet (in italics) signified to the audience that the scene was ending at a time when there was little if any scenery on stage, no curtains and no lights to dim, but the audience would recognise the significance and know a scene was ending.*

NB: If you are reading the play in the original scene order, now jump back to page 16.

ACT I SCENE III

A ROOM IN OLIVIA'S HOUSE.

ENTER SIR TOBY BELCH WEARING RIDING BOOTS*, AND MARIA CARRYING A LIGHT. (A LANTERN OR A CANDLE)*.

SIR TOBY, THE UNCLE OF THE WEALTHY COUNTESS OLIVIA, IS A LARGE, LOUD, DRUNK MAN, OVERFOND OF HIS FOOD AND DRINK.

MARIA IS A PETITE, YOUNG, PERSONAL MAID TO THE COUNTESS OLIVIA.

**Note: Sir Toby arrives in riding boots. This signifies he has just arrived at Olivia's house by horse. Maria carries a light signifying it is evening or night time.*

This scene is mostly written in prose, as opposed to the normal blank verse which is a form of poetry which doesn't rhyme except for effect. Prose is used to break the rhythm and for light-hearted and comedic characters.

The exchange between the characters is filled with sexual suggestion and innuendo, often hidden behind nautical terms.

SIR TOBY BELCH
What the devil does my niece mean in taking the death of her brother in this way? I am sure sorrow is an enemy to one's health.

SIR TOBY BELCH
What a plague means my niece to take the death of her brother thus? I am sure care's an enemy to life.

MARIA
My goodness, Sir Toby, you must visit earlier at night. Your niece, my lady, takes great exception to your late hours.

MARIA
By my troth, Sir Toby, you must come in earlier a'nights. Your cousin*, my lady, takes great exceptions to your ill hours.

**Note: 'Cousin' – relative. Cousin then meant anyone closely related.*

SIR TOBY BELCH
Then let her accept it since it is now expected.

SIR TOBY BELCH
Why, let her except before excepted.

**Note: 'Except before excepted' – a legal phrase, Shakespeare often threw in legal phrases, it means exclude (allow) things previously ordered to be excluded. The translation has a slightly different play on words but the overall effect is of Sir Toby being what he thinks is clever with his wording.*

Sir Toby is quite drunk.

MARIA
But you must confine yourself within the limits of common decency.

MARIA
Ay, but you must confine yourself within the modest limits of order.

SIR TOBY BELCH
Confine? I'll confine myself to the finery I am in. These clothes are good enough to drink in, and so are these boots too. If they are not, let them hang themselves by their own straps.

SIR TOBY BELCH
Confine? I'll confine myself no finer than I am. These clothes are good enough to drink in, and so be these boots too; and they be not, let them hang themselves in their own straps.

MARIA
This overindulgence of drink will be your undoing. I heard my lady talking about it yesterday, and about a foolish knight you brought here with you one night to woo her.

MARIA
That quaffing and drinking will undo you. I heard my lady talk of it yesterday; and of a foolish knight that you brought in one night here to be her wooer.

SIR TOBY BELCH
Who? Sir Andrew Aguecheek?

SIR TOBY BELCH
Who, Sir Andrew Aguecheek?

MARIA
Yes, him.

MARIA
Ay, he.

SIR TOBY BELCH
He's as big a man as any in Illyria.

SIR TOBY BELCH
He's as tall a man as any's in Illyria.

MARIA
And how is that useful?

MARIA
What's that to th' purpose?

SIR TOBY BELCH
Well, he earns three thousand ducats a year.

SIR TOBY BELCH
Why, he has three thousand ducats* a year.

**Note: A Ducat was a gold coin used to trade between nations. Although each country had its own design the ducat was valid everywhere due to its value in precious metal.*

Ducats are still traded today, mostly as investments, similar to gold sovereigns or Krugerrands. Shakespeare used the word a lot in his works to the point where the word 'ducat' became slang for money.

MARIA
Yes, but he'll have spent all those ducats in a year. He's a wasteful, self-indulgent fool.

MARIA
Ay, but he'll have but a year in all these ducats. He's a very fool and a prodigal.

SIR TOBY BELCH
Shame on you for saying so! He plays the cello and speaks three of four languages fluently, and has been gifted with all the finer qualities to be found in nature.

SIR TOBY BELCH
Fie that you'll say so! He plays o'th' viol-de-gamboys,* and speaks three or four languages* word for word without book, and hath all the good gifts of nature.

**Note: 'Viol-de-gamboys' - an ancient instrument related to the cello. As it is held between the legs it is often used as a sexual metaphor by Shakespeare.*

We will shortly learn that despite Sir Toby's claim, Sir Andrew does not speak any foreign languages.

MARIA
He does indeed have "all" most finer qualities, but he's a fool. He's always arguing, and if not for the gift of cowardice to counteract the relish he has for quarrelling, it's thought by those more refined that he would quickly be gifted with a grave.

MARIA
He hath indeed "all" most* natural*; for, besides that he's a fool, he's a great quarreller; and but that he hath the gift of a coward to allay the gust he hath in quarrelling, 'tis thought among the prudent he would quickly have the gift of a grave.

**Note: 'All most' – she plays on the words sounding like 'almost'. i.e. he almost has the finer qualities but he's an idiot. 'Natural' – an idiot.*

SIR TOBY BELCH
On my oath…

SIR TOBY BELCH
By this hand,

HE RAISES HIS HAND AS IF SWEARING AN OATH.

SIR TOBY BELCH (CONT'D)
…those that say so are scoundrels and 'subtractors'. Who are they?

SIR TOBY BELCH
they are scoundrels and substractors* that say so of him. Who are they?

**Note: 'Substractors' – Sir Toby drunkenly mispronounces 'detractors'.*

MARIA
Those, who in 'addition', say he's drunk with you every night.

MARIA
They that add*, moreover, he's drunk nightly in your company.

**Note: 'Add' – playing on Sir Toby's previous mispronunciation 'substractors'.*

SIR TOBY BELCH
(*indignant*) With the drinking of toasts to my niece. I'll drink to her as long as my throat is able and there is still drink in Illyria. He might be a coward who brags, but he will drink a toast to my niece until his brains turn topsy-turvy like a merry-go-round. What are you saying, wench! Talk of the devil, here comes Sir Andrew Agueface now.

SIR TOBY BELCH
With drinking healths to my niece. I'll drink to her as long as there is a passage in my throat and drink in Illyria. He's a coward and a coistrel* that will not drink to my niece till his brains turn o'th' toe like a parish top. What, wench! Castiliano vulgo;* for here comes Sir Andrew Agueface.*

**Note: 'Coistrel' – a man who carries the arms of barons and knights. Meaning here that he carries arms but is too much of a coward to use them. For show only.*

'Castiliano vulgo' – the meaning of this phrase is not known, it seems to be a warning to Maria that the man they are talking about is approaching.

'Agueface' – His name is Aguecheek. Whether this was a drunken error or he is insulting the man's name is not known.

ENTER SIR ANDREW AGUECHEEK, THE MAN THEY ARE TALKING ABOUT.

SIR ANDREW AGUECHEEK Sir Toby Belch! How are you, Sir Toby Belch?	SIR ANDREW AGUECHEEK Sir Toby Belch! How now, Sir Toby Belch?
SIR TOBY BELCH Dearest Sir Andrew!	SIR TOBY BELCH Sweet Sir Andrew!

THE TWO MEN EMBRACE. SIR TOBY IS FAT, SIR ANDREW IS THIN.

SIR ANDREW AGUECHEEK (*to Maria*) Bless you, pretty mouse.	SIR ANDREW AGUECHEEK Bless you, fair shrew*.

**Note: 'Shrew' – an ill-tempered woman. A shrew-mouse was probably the double-meaning here regarding Maria's petite stature, which is addressed later.*

MARIA And you too, sir.	MARIA And you too, sir.

SIR TOBY NUDGES SIR ANDREW SUGGESTIVELY.

SIR TOBY BELCH Accost, Sir Andrew, accost her.	SIR TOBY BELCH Accost, Sir Andrew, accost* her.

**Note: 'Accost' – a nautical term meaning to go alongside. It also means to approach someone forcefully.*

Sir Toby means that Sir Andrew should introduce himself to Maria properly with suggestive undertones. Sir Andrew mistakes 'accost' for her surname.

SIR ANDREW AGUECHEEK Who's that?	SIR ANDREW AGUECHEEK What's that?

SIR TOBY DRUNKENLY WINKS AT SIR ANDREW
AND NODS IN MARIA'S DIRECTION..

SIR TOBY BELCH My niece's chambermaid.	SIR TOBY BELCH My niece's chambermaid.*

**Note: 'Chambermaid' – he demotes her to a lower position than she actually has.*

SIR TOBY ONCE AGAIN NUDGES SIR ANDREW.

SIR ANDREW MISUNDERSTANDS HIS MEANING, ASSUMING IT IS HER NAME.

SIR ANDREW AGUECHEEK My good Mistress Accost, I desire to better make your acquaintance.	SIR ANDREW AGUECHEEK Good Mistress Accost, I desire better acquaintance.

MARIA
(*indignant*) My name is Mary, sir.

MARIA
My name is Mary, sir.

**Note:* *'Mary' – her name is Maria. There is a lot of confusion with names throughout the play, whether this is deliberate is not known, many essays have been written on the subject.*

SIR ANDREW AGUECHEEK
My good Mistress Mary Accost…

SIR TOBY BELCH
(*interrupting*) You're mistaken, sir knight. "Accost' means, approach her, broadside her, woo her, launch an attack.

SIR ANDREW AGUECHEEK
Good Mistress Mary Accost -

SIR TOBY BELCH
You mistake, knight. "Accost" is front her*, board her*, woo* her, assail* her.

**Note:* *'Front her' – approach or confront her. A series of nautical terms as metaphors for sexual advances to further the nautical meaning behind 'accost'.*

'Board her' – come alongside or attack and forcefully board an enemy ship in nautical terms, as well as the more obvious climb on board.

'Woo' – win favour with, seduce. There seems to be no nautical use of the word woo, making this the odd one out.

'Assail' – assault or attempt to seduce

SIR ANDREW AGUECHEEK
Upon my oath, I would not confront her in present company.

SIR ANDREW AGUECHEEK
By my troth, I would not undertake her in this company.

SIR ANDREW INDICATES THE AUDIENCE, COMICALLY.

SIR ANDREW AGUECHEEK (CONT'D)
(*in confidence to Sir Toby*) Is that the meaning of "accost"?

SIR ANDREW AGUECHEEK
Is that the meaning of "accost"?

MARIA TURNS TO LEAVE.

MARIA
I bid you farewell, gentlemen.

SIR TOBY BELCH
(*to Sir Andrew*) If you let her go without confronting her, Sir Andrew, may you never draw your <u>sword</u> again.

MARIA
Fare you well, gentlemen.

SIR TOBY BELCH
And thou let part so, Sir Andrew, would thou mightst never draw sword* again.

**Note:* *'Draw sword' – a pun on not being a man and sword as an innuendo for penis.*

HAVING BEEN CHALLENGED BY SIR TOBY TO SEDUCE MARIA,
SIR ANDREW CALLS TO MARIA TO PREVENT HER LEAVING.

SIR ANDREW AGUECHEEK
If you leave now, mistress, may I never draw my sword again. Beautiful lady, do you think you are handling fools?

SIR ANDREW AGUECHEEK
And you part so, mistress, I would I might never draw sword again. Fair lady, do you think you have fools in hand?

MARIA
Sir, I am not handling you.

MARIA
Sir, I have not you by th' hand.

SIR ANDREW AGUECHEEK
Oh, but you shall. Here's my hand.

SIR ANDREW AGUECHEEK
Marry, but you shall have; and here's my hand.

**Note: 'Marry' – by (the virgin) Mary, a mild expletive. All plays were vetted before they could be performed for obscenity, blasphemy and anti-royal content.*

SIR ANDREW HOLDS OUT HIS HAND TO MARIA WHO TAKES IT IN HERS.

MARIA
Well, sir, you can think what you like. I suggest you bring your hand to the buttery-bar, and let it drink.

MARIA
Now, sir, thought is free. I pray you bring your hand to th' buttery-bar*, and let it drink.

**Note: 'Buttery-bar' – the ledge of a hatch through which drink is served – with the innuendo that her bosom also forms a ledge. A buttery is the place where butts (barrels) of ale and wine are kept.*

Shakespeare put in no stage direction at this point, but many productions emphasise the innuendoes by Maria placing his hand on her bosom.

The Buttery-Bar

SIR ANDREW AGUECHEEK
Why, sweetheart? What are you suggesting?

SIR ANDREW AGUECHEEK
Wherefore, sweetheart? What's your metaphor?

MARIA
It's dry, sir.

MARIA
It's dry, sir.

MARIA LOOKS DOWN AT HIS HAND.

SIR ANDREW AGUECHEEK
I should think so. I am not such an ass that I can't keep my hand dry. What's your witticism?

SIR ANDREW AGUECHEEK
Why, I think so. I am not such an ass but I can keep my hand dry. But what's your jest?

MARIA
A dry wit, sir.

MARIA
A dry jest, sir.

SIR ANDREW AGUECHEEK
Are you full of them?

SIR ANDREW AGUECHEEK
Are you full of them?

MARIA
Yes, sir, I have them at my fingertips.

MARIA
Ay, sir, I have them at my fingers' ends.

SHE BACKS AWAY FROM HIM SO HE JUST HOLDS HER FINGER TIPS.
SHE PAUSES THEN PULLS HER HAND AWAY COMPLETELY.

MARIA
Goodness, now I release your hand, I am barren.

MARIA
Marry, now I let go your hand, I am barren.*

**Note: 'Barren' – empty, without. Triple meaning of no longer having his hand, no longer having any jests, and suggestive of being childless, therefore unmarried.*

MARIA TURNS AND LEAVES.

SIR TOBY TAKES PITY ON SIR ANDREW FOR FAILING IN HIS TASK.

SIR TOBY BELCH
(*sympathetically*) Oh, sir knight, you're in need of a glass of Madeira.

SIR TOBY BELCH
O knight, thou lack'st a cup of canary*.

**Note: 'Canary' – fortified sweet wine from the Canary Islands. Popular in Elizabethan England amongst aristocracy though production ceased suddenly in the 1680s. Madeira wine is made from the same grapes and is the closest we have today, its strength is 20% alcohol. It is also similar to sweet sherry.*

SIR TOBY POURS TWO GLASSES OF WINE. HE HANDS ONE TO SIR ANDREW.

SIR TOBY BELCH (CONT'D)
When did I ever see you put down like this?

SIR ANDREW AGUECHEEK
Never in your life, I think, unless you've seen Madeira put me down on the floor. I think sometimes I have no more wits about me than a monk or a commoner. But I am a great eater of beef, and I believe that does harm to my wit.

SIR TOBY BELCH
Without question.

SIR ANDREW AGUECHEEK
If it does, I'll give it up.
– I'm riding home tomorrow, Sir Toby.

SIR TOBY BELCH
Pourquoi, my dear knight?

SIR TOBY BELCH
When did I see thee so put down?

SIR ANDREW AGUECHEEK
Never in your life, I think, unless you see canary put me down. Methinks sometimes I have no more wit than a Christian or an ordinary man has. But I am a great eater of beef, and I believe that does harm to my wit.

SIR TOBY BELCH
No question.

SIR ANDREW AGUECHEEK
And I thought that, I'd forswear it. I'll ride home tomorrow, Sir Toby.

SIR TOBY BELCH
Pourquoi,* my dear knight?

**Note: 'Pourquoi' – French for 'why'.*

SIR ANDREW AGUECHEEK
What does "pourquoi" mean? Go, or not go? I wish I'd spent the time studying foreign tongues that I've spent fencing, dancing, and bear-baiting. Oh, if only I'd studied the arts.

SIR ANDREW AGUECHEEK
What is "pourquoi"? - do, or not do? I would I had bestowed that time in the tongues that I have in fencing*, dancing, and bear-baiting*. O, had I but followed the arts!

**Note: 'Fencing' – the sport of fighting with swords.*

**'Bear-baiting' was once a common blood sport. It is known there was a bear used for such purposes near the Globe Theatre and Shakespeare wrote the bear into plays. The 'sport' comprised a bear chained to a stake upon which dogs (usually Old English Bulldogs) were set loose to 'bait' it – attack it, forcing it to defend itself. A 'course' was a single session, like a 'round' in boxing, where the bear had no option but to fight or be killed. It was outlawed in 1835 under Parliament's Cruelty To Animals Act .*

Bear Baiting With Dogs

SIR TOBY BELCH
And with those 'tongs' you'd have had a fine head of hair.

SIR TOBY BELCH
Then hadst thou had an excellent head of hair.

**Note: Sir Toby has twisted the word 'tongues' by Sir Andrew into 'tongs' used for curling hair. Back then the two words were pronounced the same way.*

SIR ANDREW AGUECHEEK
Would they have fixed my hair?

SIR ANDREW AGUECHEEK
Why, would that have mended my hair?

SIR ANDREW RUNS HIS FINGERS THROUGH HIS LONG, LANK HAIR, SELF-CONSCIOUSLY.

SIR TOBY BELCH
Beyond doubt. You can see it doesn't curl naturally.

SIR TOBY BELCH
Past question, for thou seest it will not curl by nature.

SIR ANDREW AGUECHEEK
It suits me well enough though, doesn't it?

SIR ANDREW AGUECHEEK
But it becomes me well enough, does't not?

SIR TOBY BELCH
Very well, it hangs like unspun wool, and I wish a hussy would take you between her legs and spin it out.

SIR TOBY BELCH
Excellent; it hangs like flax* on a distaff*, and I hope to see a huswife* take thee between her legs and spin it off*.

**Note: 'Flax on a distaff' – women spun flax or wool to make clothing with. The 'distaff', also known as a spindle, was a long thin pole the raw wool was wound around. Before the spinning wheel replaced this method in 1850 (though versions of the spinning wheel had been around for centuries in other countries) women would spin (twist) the wool by hand, with the pole held between their legs.*

'Housewife' – until the 17th century the original meaning of housewife was an immoral woman. Hussy is a contraction of the word. Housewifery was attending to the duties of the household – housework.

'Spin it off' – there are suggestions this referred to catching syphilis from a prostitute, one of the symptoms being the hair falling out, or it could be a simple sexual innuendo.

Hand Spinning Wool

SIR ANDREW AGUECHEEK
Anyway, I'm returning home tomorrow, Sir Toby. Your niece will not see me, or if she does, it's a good bet she'll have nothing to do with me. The neighbouring count himself tries his hardest to gain her affections.

SIR ANDREW AGUECHEEK
Faith, I'll home tomorrow, Sir Toby. Your niece will not be seen; or if she be, it's four to one she'll none of me. The count* himself here hard by woos her.

SIR TOBY BELCH
She'll have nothing to do with the count. She won't marry above her rank, whether in wealth, age or intelligence, I've heard her swear to it. So, there's hope for you, man.

SIR TOBY BELCH
She'll none o'th' count.* She'll not match above her degree, neither in estate, years, nor wit; I have heard her swear't. Tut, there's life in't, man.

**Note: 'Count' – He refers to Duke Orsini who is not a count, however the second occurrence of the word can be delivered in such a way as if to sound like an expletive. The confusion in titles occurs frequently throughout the play. From what he says, we can deduce that the Duke is older than Olivia, and that Sir Andrew is roughly the same age.*

SIR ANDREW AGUECHEEK
(*comedic change of mind*) I think I'll stay another month. I'm a fellow with the strangest quirks in behaviour. I adore masquerades and making merry, sometimes at the same time.

SIR ANDREW AGUECHEEK
I'll stay a month longer. I am a fellow o'th' strangest mind i'th' world: I delight in masques and revels sometimes altogether.

SIR TOBY BELCH
Are you proficient at these petit trifles, sir?

SIR TOBY BELCH
Art thou good at these kickshawses, knight?

**Note: 'Kickshawses' – trifles. Corruption of the French 'quelque chose' (something).*

SIR ANDREW AGUECHEEK
As any man in Illyria of lesser standing than my superiors, whatever the man may be – though not so proficient as an old man.

SIR ANDREW AGUECHEEK
As any man in Illyria, whatsoever he be, under the degree of my betters; and yet I will not compare with an old man.

SIR TOBY BELCH
How proficient are you at dancing, sir knight?

SIR TOBY BELCH
What is thy excellence in a galliard*, knight?

SIR ANDREW AGUECHEEK
Truly, I can cut a merry caper.

SIR ANDREW AGUECHEEK
Faith, I can cut a caper*.

**Note: 'Galliard' – a lively dance of four steps and a leap. The leap known as a 'caper'.*

Dances with frolicsome leaps (capers) were popular in Elizabethan England among the nobility. It is from this we get 'Ten lords a-leaping' in the Twelve Days Of Christmas song.

'Cut a caper' – perform the leap with confidence. Caper is also a pickled flower bud, which is the meaning Sir Toby assumes with his next line. Today we say cut the mustard, meaning good or with added spice/zest. 'Mutton' was also slang for a whore.

SIR TOBY BELCH
And I can cut the mutton to go with it.

SIR TOBY BELCH
And I can cut the mutton* to't.

SIR ANDREW AGUECHEEK
And I think I can do the backwards leap as well as any man in Illyria.

SIR ANDREW AGUECHEEK
And I think I have the back-trick simply as strong as any man in Illyria.

SIR TOBY BELCH
Why are these talents hidden? Why do these gifts have a veil around them? Are they likely to gather dust, like Mistress Mall's picture?

SIR TOBY BELCH
Wherefore are these things hid? Wherefore have these gifts a curtain* before 'em?* Are they like to take dust, like Mistress Mall's* picture?

**Note: 'Curtain' – valuable paintings had curtains in front of them to keep off dust and prevent fading.*

'Mistress Mall' – It has long been assumed that this was the notorious singing, dancing, lute playing, cross-dressing, pickpocket and criminal fence known as Moll Cutpurse. However she was only seventeen when Shakespeare wrote this play and had not yet reached her notoriety. It could be just a comparison to a curtained painting and Olivia now wearing a veil to hide her face, using a generic name, like Jane Doe, as the subject of the painting was covered and therefore unknown.

SIR TOBY BELCH (CONT'D)
Why don't you quick-step your way to church and come home with a waltz? If it was me my walk would be a jig. I would even pass water in a sink-at-pace. I ask you! Is this a world to hide your qualities in? By the excellent constitution of your leg I thought it must be born under a dancing star.

SIR TOBY BELCH
Why dost thou not go to church in a galliard and come home in a coranto? My very walk should be a jig; I would not so much as make water but in a cinquepace*. What dost thou mean? Is it a world to hide virtues in? I did think, by the excellent constitution of thy leg, it was formed under the star of a galliard.

**Note: 'Cinquepace' – a five step lively dance, he phonetically says it as English words.*

SIR ANDREW AGUECHEEK
Aye, it's sturdy, and it looks moderately good in a brightly coloured stocking.
– Shall we start some revelling?

SIR ANDREW AGUECHEEK
Ay, 'tis strong, and it does indifferent well in a damned-coloured* stock. Shall we set about some revels?

**Note: 'Dam'd coloured' – as it was originally spelt in early texts. There have been endless arguments about what this means, going by the nature of Sir Andrew it was probably extravagantly coloured in some form. Some editions say 'flame coloured'.*

SIR TOBY BELCH
What else should we do? Weren't we born under the sign of Taurus?

SIR TOBY BELCH
What shall we do else? Were we not born under Taurus?

SIR ANDREW AGUECHEEK
Taurus? That's the sign for sides and hearts.

SIR ANDREW AGUECHEEK
Taurus?* - that's sides and heart.

SIR TOBY BELCH
No, sir, it is for legs and thighs. Let me see you caper about.

SIR TOBY BELCH
No, sir, it is legs and thighs. Let me see thee caper.

**Note: 'Taurus' – they are both wrong, probably deliberately for comedic effect, Taurus is the sign for the neck and throat, appropriate for drinkers.*

SIR ANDREW LEAPS INTO THE AIR WITHOUT ANY ELEGANCE.

SIR TOBY BELCH (CONT'D)
Ha, higher!

SIR TOBY BELCH
Ha, higher!

SIR ANDREW LEAPS AGAIN ALMOST FALLING OVER AS HE LANDS.

SIR TOBY BELCH (CONT'D)
Ha, ha, excellent!

SIR TOBY BELCH
Ha, ha, excellent!

ACT I SCENE IV

A ROOM IN THE DUKE'S PALACE.

ENTER VALENTINE, A PRETENTIOUS PERSONAL ATTENDANT TO THE DUKE, AND VIOLA DISGUISED AND DRESSED AS A YOUNG MAN NOW CALLED CESARIO.

Note: Viola may have her hair cut short or she may tuck it under a cap.

VALENTINE
If the Duke '*continues*' to show you such favour, Cesario, you are likely to go far in his household. He has known you only three days and already you are close companions.

VALENTINE
If the duke continue these favours towards you, Cesario, you are like to be much advanced. He hath known you but three days, and already you are no stranger.

VIOLA (AS CESARIO)
If you call into question the '*continuation*' of his favour towards me I suspect you either fear his mood swings or that I'll be negligent in my duties. Is he inconstant in his moods, sir?

VIOLA
You either fear his humour or my negligence, that you call in question the continuance of his love. Is he inconstant, sir, in his favours?

VALENTINE
(*sarcastic*) Believe me, no.

VALENTINE
No, believe me.

ENTER DUKE ORSINO, ACCOMPANIED BY CURIO, WHO IS ANOTHER PERSONAL ATTENDANT TO THE DUKE, AND ATTENDANTS.

VIOLA (AS CESARIO)
I thank you. Here comes the count now.

VIOLA
I thank you. Here comes the count*.

**Note: Again the confusion between being a count or a duke.*

DUKE ORSINO
Has anyone seen Cesario, huh?

DUKE ORSINO
Who saw Cesario, ho?

VIOLA (AS CESARIO) STEPS FORWARD AND BOWS.

VIOLA (AS CESARIO)
Here, at your service, my lord.

VIOLA
On your attendance, my lord, here.

DUKE ORSINO INDICATES HIS ATTENDANTS AS HE GIVES AN ORDER FOR THEM TO STAND AWAY AT A DISTANCE.

DUKE ORSINO
(*to attendants*) Stand aside for a while.

DUKE ORSINO
Stand you awhile aloof.

CURIO AND ATTENDANTS STAND TO THE SIDE, JEALOUS OF THE ATTENTION VIOLA IS RECEIVING FROM THEIR MASTER.

DUKE ORSINO TAKES VIOLA (AS CESARIO) INTO HIS CONFIDENCE OUT OF EARSHOT OF THE OTHERS.

DUKE ORSINO (CONT'D)
(*to Viola alone*) You know everything about me, I have opened my heart and soul to you. Therefore, young man, go directly to her. Do not allow her to deny you access. Stand at her door and tell them you will take root there until you have spoken with her.

DUKE ORSINO
Thou know'st no less but all: I have unclasped
To thee the book even of my secret soul.
Therefore, good youth, address thy gait unto her;
Be not denied access, stand at her doors,
And tell them there thy fixed foot shall grow
Till thou have audience.

VIOLA (AS CESARIO)
Surely, my noble lord, if she is as lost in her sorrows as people say, she will never allow me admittance.

VIOLA
Sure, my noble lord,
If she be so abandoned to her sorrow
As it is spoke, she never will admit me.

DUKE ORSINO
Protest loudly, make a nuisance of yourself, don't come back unsatisfied.

DUKE ORSINO
Be clamorous, and leap all civil bounds,
Rather than make unprofited return.

VIOLA (AS CESARIO)
What if I do speak with her, my lord, what then?

VIOLA
Say I do speak with her, my lord, what then?

DUKE ORSINO
Oh, then you must reveal how passionate my love is. Surprise her with talk of my dear affection. It would be good if you could enact my sorrow. She will take better notice from a youth than from an aged messenger's solemn manner

DUKE ORSINO
O, then unfold the passion of my love,
Surprise her with discourse of my dear faith.
It shall become thee well to act my woes:
She will attend it better in thy youth
Than in a nuncio's of more grave aspect.

THE DUKE SCOWLS OVER AT VALENTINE, SHOWING WHO HE MEANT.

VALENTINE STICKS HIS NOSE UP IN THE AIR IN DISDAIN.

VIOLA (AS CESARIO)
I don't think so, my lord.

VIOLA
I think not so, my lord.

DUKE ORSINO

Dear boy, believe it, anyone who treats you as a man deprives you of the happiness of youth. The goddess Diana's lip is no more smooth and rosy than yours. Your small pipe is like a maiden's organ, shrill and unbroken, it resembles that of a woman. I know your character is right for this affair.

DUKE ORSINO

Dear lad, believe it;
For they shall yet belie thy happy years
That say thou art a man. Diana's* lip
Is not more smooth and rubious*; thy small pipe*
Is as the maiden's organ*, shrill and sound,
And all is semblative a woman's part*.
I know thy constellation is right apt
For this affair.

**Note: The Duke's speech is full of innuendo, and in humorous fashion he is saying Viola, being so young, resembles a woman, so will be received better by Olivia than one of his aged male attendants. The audience knows Viola is a woman, but Orsino doesn't.*

'Diana' - goddess of women and chastity, suggesting innocence.

'Rubious' – ruby-red.

'Small Pipe' – shrill voice, with the innuendo of small penis.
A small musical pipe was very high pitched and shrill.

'Maiden's organ' – a virgin's voice, with the innuendo of her sexual organ.

'Woman's part' – a female quality with again the innuendo on her genitals.

THE DUKE TURNS TO HIS ATTENDANTS WHO ARE STANDING ASIDE.

DUKE ORSINO (CONT'D)

(*to Attendants*) Four or five of you accompany him. – No, all of you would be better, I feel best when I'm alone.
(*to Viola*) Succeed in this and you will live as freely as I, your master, and share in his good fortune.

DUKE ORSINO

[*To Attendants.*] Some four or five attend him;
All, if you will; for I myself am best
When least in company. Prosper well in this
And thou shalt live as freely as thy lord
To call his fortunes thine.

VIOLA (AS CESARIO)

I'll do my best to woo your lady.
(*aside as the Duke exits*)
This is a conflict full of woeful strife!
I woo for him, but wish I were his wife.

VIOLA

I'll do my best
To woo your lady. [Aside.] Yet a barful strife!
*Whoe'er I woo, myself would be his wife.**

**Note: Did you spot the rhyming couplet to notify the end of a scene?*

A rhyming couplet could also be used in the middle of a scene when a major character was about to make an exit.

Rhyming couplets were not used at the end of every scene. If it was obvious there was a scene change they could be omitted.

ACT I SCENE V

A Room In Olivia's House.

Enter Maria and Feste the Clown (a comedian)

Maria is chastising Feste the jester.

MARIA
Now, either tell me where you have been, or I will close my lips so tightly a bristle may not pass through them to utter an excuse for you. My lady will hang you for your absence.

MARIA
Nay, either tell me where thou hast been, or I will not open my lips so wide as a bristle may enter in way of thy excuse. My lady will hang thee for thy absence.

FESTE
Let her hang me. A man well hanged in this world fears no colours.

FESTE
Let her hang me. He that is well hanged in this world needs to fear no colours.*

Note: 'Fear no colours' – a military saying which Maria explains later, with a pun on the words 'collar' (noose) and 'colour', and the innuendo on well hung.

MARIA
Explain the meaning of that.

MARIA
Make that good.

FESTE
He will not see any to fear.

FESTE
He shall see none to fear.

MARIA
A good non-answer. I can tell you where the saying "I fear no colours" comes from.

MARIA
A good Lenten* answer. I can tell thee where that saying was born, of "I fear no colours".

**Note: 'Lenten' – sparce. From the Christian period of fasting known as Lent, which ends with Easter and starts on Shrove Tuesday (also known as pancake day or Mardi Gras). In the bible, Jesus spent forty days and forty nights surviving the temptations of Satan in the wilderness, Christians acknowledge this today by giving up certain luxuries for the same period of time.*

FESTE
Where, good Mistress Mary?

FESTE
Where, good Mistress Mary?

MARIA
From the wars. Armies display their colours in battle. And if in future you should be so bold as to say so in your tomfoolery.

MARIA
In the wars; and that may you be bold to say in your foolery.

Note: An ensign carrying the colours of the Buckinghamshire Militia, 1793.

FESTE	FESTE
Well, God give wisdom to those that are wise, and to those that are fools, let them use their skills wisely.	Well, God give them wisdom that have it; and those that are fools, let them use their talents.*

**Note: Feste has inverted the saying - God give wisdom to those that have none, and those that are wise let them put their skills to good use.*

MARIA	MARIA
You'll be hanged for being absent so long, or you'll be thrown out - which is as good as being hanged to you, isn't it?	Yet you will be hanged for being so long absent; or to be turned away - is not that as good as a hanging to you?
FESTE	FESTE
Often a good hanging prevents a bad marriage, as for being thrown out, I can endure the summer.	Many a good hanging* prevents a bad marriage*; and for turning away, let summer bear it out

**Note: 'Good hanging' - A second deliberate pun on being well hung (large penis).*

There was also an often retold story of the time about a condemned criminal whose life was begged for by a female if he would marry her. Upon viewing his intended bride when out on the cart to be taken to the gallows to be hanged, all he said was 'drive on, carter'.

MARIA	MARIA
Your mind's made up then?	You are resolute then?
FESTE	FESTE
No, I wouldn't say that, but I am tied between two points.	Not so, neither; but I am resolved on two points*.

HE HOOKS HIS THUMBS IN HIS BRACES AND PULLS THE STRAPS FORWARD IN EMPHASIS.

**Note: 'Points' – laces or cords used to hold up 'gaskins' (pants or trousers). He is setting up a joke which Maria has heard so she says the punch line, ruining it for him. In the UK they would be similar to braces, in the USA, suspenders.*

MARIA	MARIA
(*interrupts*) And if one breaks, the other will hold. Or if both break your breeches fall down.	That if one break, the other will hold; or if both break, your gaskins* fall.
FESTE	FESTE
(*laughing*) Good, in all honesty, very good. Well, get along. If Sir Toby would stop drinking you would be as witty a piece of female flesh for him as any in Illyria.	Apt, in good faith, very apt. Well, go thy way. If Sir Toby would leave drinking thou wert as witty a piece of Eve's flesh as any in Illyria.

MARIA BLUSHES AND HITS HIS ARM IN EMBARRASSMENT.

MARIA
Enough, you rogue, I'll hear no more of that.

MARIA
Peace, you rogue, no more o' that.

MARIA NOTICES OLIVIA APPROACHING.

MARIA (CONT'D)
(*seeing Olivia approaching*) Here comes my lady. You'd best have some good excuses ready, if you know what's good for you.

MARIA
Here comes my lady. Make your excuse wisely, you were best.

MARIA SCURRIES AWAY.

ENTER LADY OLIVIA, DRESSED IN BLACK AND WEARING A VEIL, ACCOMPANIED BY MALVOLIO AND ATTENDANTS.

FESTE, THE CLOWN, PUTS HIS HANDS TOGETHER AS IF IN PRAYER.

FESTE
(*in pretend prayer*) Wit, if it is your will, may my fooling go down well. Those wits that think they have you often prove to be fools, and me, who I know lacks you, may I pass for a wise man. What does Quinapalus say on this? "Better a witty fool that a foolish wit".
(*to Olivia*) God bless you, Lady!

FESTE
Wit, and't be thy will, put me into good fooling. Those wits that think they have thee do very oft prove fools, and I that am sure I lack thee may pass for a wise man. For what says Quinapalus?* "Better a witty fool than a foolish wit." God bless thee, lady!

**Note: 'Quinapalus' – for centuries scholars have pondered about this non-existent philosopher whose name Shakespeare invented. It has more recently been suggested the name was created by using the Elizabethan craze of the time of making anagrams. They used slightly different rules so they are not perfect anagrams to us. Queen Elizabeth I, who the show was first performed to, was a huge fan of them. By Elizabethan rules it is an anagram of "Aquinas" and "Paul". In the bible Paul said 'If any man among you seems to be wise in this world, let him become a fool' (and many other things about fools). The philosopher Aquinas identified twenty different types of fools and referred to Paul's writings on fools.*

LADY OLIVIA TURNS AND ADDRESSES HER ATTENDANTS.

LADY OLIVIA
(*to attendants*) Take the fool away.

FESTE
Did you hear her, gents? Take the lady away.

LADY OLIVIA
Stop that, your foolishness has run dry. I'll have no more of you. And besides, you are becoming untrustworthy.

LADY OLIVIA
Take the fool away.

FESTE
Do you not hear, fellows? Take away the lady.

LADY OLIVIA
Go to, y'are a dry fool; I'll no more of you. Besides, you grow dishonest.

FESTE
Two faults, madonna, that drink and wise words will amend. If you give the dry fool a drink, then the fool is not dry. Tell the untrustworthy man to mend his ways, if he mends, he is no longer untrustworthy, if he cannot, then let the patcher mend him. Anything that's mended, is merely patched over. Good behaviour that has erred has been temporarily patched over with sin, and sin that is corrected is likewise patched over with goodness. If this simple reasoning is good, so be it, if it is not, what can be done? In life there are always mishaps, but like a flower's beauty they don't last.

FESTE
Two faults, madonna*, that drink and good counsel will amend; for give the dry fool drink, then is the fool not dry; bid the dishonest man mend himself, if he mend, he is no longer dishonest; if he cannot, let the botcher mend him. Anything that's mended is but patched: virtue that transgresses is but patched with sin, and sin that amends is but patched with virtue. If that this simple syllogism* will serve, so; if it will not, what remedy? As there is no true cuckold but calamity, so beauty's a flower.

**Note:* 'Madonna' – *Italian for 'my lady'.*

'Botcher' – a person that repaired clothing, often by using patches. A fool's outfit consisted of patches of different colour and pattern sewed together.

'Syllogism' – deductive reasoning that reaches a conclusion which may not be correct. He uses syllogism throughout the play. An example of a syllogism that reaches an incorrect conclusion is; All dogs are mammals, cats are mammals, therefore all dogs are cats.

FESTE TURNS TO THE ATTENDANTS.

FESTE (CONT'D)
The lady ordered you to take away the fool. Therefore I repeat, take her away.

LADY OLIVIA
Sir, I ordered them to take you away.

FESTE
Falsely accused in the highest degree! Madam, *cucullus non facit monachum* – that's like saying "I wear fool's clothes but I'm not a fool in the head". Good madonna, allow me to prove *you* are the fool.

FESTE
The lady bade take away the fool, therefore I say again, take her away.

LADY OLIVIA
Sir, I bade them take away you.

FESTE
Misprision in the highest degree! Lady, cucullus non facit monachum - that's as much to say as "I wear not motley in my brain." Good madonna, give me leave to prove you a fool.

**Note: 'Cucullus non facit monachum' – wearing a hood does not make a man a monk.*

LADY OLIVIA
Can you do that?

FESTE
With great 'dextererity', good madonna.

LADY OLIVIA
Can you do it?

FESTE
Dexteriously*, good madonna.

**Note: 'Dexteriously' – he mispronounces dexterously in a grandiose way.*

LADY OLIVIA
Present your proof.

LADY OLIVIA
Make your proof.

FESTE
I must cross-examine you to prove it, madonna. My good virtuous mouse, answer me.

FESTE
I must catechize* you for it, madonna. Good my mouse* of virtue, answer me.

**Note: 'Catechize' – religious questioning from a priest from which a person gains knowledge through their answering, it also means to interrogate someone.*

'Mouse' – used as a term of endearment for a gentle and quiet lady, in contrast to the shrew-mouse Maria was called earlier, Maria being not so quiet and gentle.

LADY OLIVIA
Well, sir, as I have no other trivial matters to attend, I'll await your proof.

LADY OLIVIA
Well, sir, for want of other idleness, I'll bide your proof.

FESTE
Good madonna, why do you mourn so deeply?

FESTE
Good madonna, why mourn'st thou?

LADY OLIVIA
Good fool, for the death of my brother.

LADY OLIVIA
Good fool, for my brother's death.

FESTE
I think his soul is in hell, madonna.

FESTE
I think his soul is in hell, madonna.

LADY OLIVIA
I know his soul is in heaven, fool.

LADY OLIVIA
I know his soul is in heaven, fool.

FESTE
How foolish, madonna, to mourn for your brother's soul if it is in heaven.

FESTE
The more fool, madonna, to mourn for your brother's soul being in heaven.

FESTE TURNS TO THE ATTENDANTS AND INDICATES OLIVIA.

FESTE (CONT'D)
Take away the fool, gentlemen.

FESTE
Take away the fool, gentlemen.

LADY OLIVIA LAUGHS.

LADY OLIVIA
(*to Malvolio, laughing*) What do you think of this fool, Malvolio? Is he not mending?

LADY OLIVIA
What think you of this fool, Malvolio? Doth he not mend?

**Note: 'Mend' – relating to Feste's speech about mending faults by patching over them.*

MALVOLIO
(*sarcastic*) Yes, and shall continue till the pangs of death take him. Old age reduces wisdom, which always makes for a better fool.

MALVOLIO
Yes, and shall do till the pangs of death shake him. Infirmity, that decays the wise, doth ever make the better fool.

FESTE
Then God send you a speedy old age, sir, to increase your foolishness! Sir Toby will swear that I am not a cunning fox, but he would not swear for twopence that you are not foolish.

FESTE
God send you, sir, a speedy infirmity, for the better increasing your folly! Sir Toby will be sworn that I am no fox, but he will not pass his word for twopence* that you are no fool.

**Note: 'Twopence' – pronounced tuppence. Two old pennies.*

LADY OLIVIA
What do you say to that Malvolio?

LADY OLIVIA
How say you to that, Malvolio?

MALVOLIO
I marvel that your ladyship takes delight in such an unamusing rascal. I saw him outclassed the other day by an unremarkable fool who had no more brains than a stone.

MALVOLIO
I marvel your ladyship takes delight in such a barren rascal. I saw him put down the other day with an ordinary fool that has no more brain than a stone.

FESTE SHRUGS HIS SHOULDERS AND TURNS AWAY AS IF UNINTERESTED.

MALVOLIO (CONT'D)
Look at him now, he's nothing to say. Unless you laugh and pander to him he is silenced. I swear these supposedly wise men who laugh so much at these repetitive fools are no better than the fools' stooges.

MALVOLIO
Look you now, he's out of his guard already; unless you laugh and minister occasion to him, he is gagged. I protest I take these wise men that crow so at these set kind of fools no better than the fools' zanies*.

**Note: 'Zanies' – minor comic assistants to the main comedy artists in Italy.*

LADY OLIVIA
Oh, you are full of your own self-importance, Malvolio, and you judge with bitter taste. To be generous, free of guilt, and unbiased, is to view these things as small pellets, not cannon balls as you do. There is nothing hurtful in a professional fool, even though he does nothing but hurl abuse, just as there is nothing hurtful meant from a more reserved (*she indicates Malvolio*) man even though he does nothing but voice his disapproval.

LADY OLIVIA
O, you are sick of self-love, Malvolio, and taste with a distempered appetite. To be generous, guiltless, and of free disposition, is to take those things for bird-bolts that you deem cannon bullets. There is no slander in an allowed fool, though he do nothing but rail; nor no railing in a known discreet man, though he do nothing but reprove.

FESTE
The god of deception must have endowed you with the power of lying, because you are speaking well of fools.

FESTE
Now Mercury endue thee with leasing, for thou speak'st well of fools.

RE-ENTER MARIA.

MARIA
Madam, there is a young gentleman at the door who greatly desires to speak with you.

LADY OLIVIA
From Count Orsini, is he?

MARIA
I don't know madam. He's a fine looking young man, with many attendants.

LADY OLIVIA
Which of my people is preventing his entry?

MARIA
Your uncle, Sir Toby, madam.

LADY OLIVIA
Call him off, I beg you, he talks nothing but nonsense. A curse on him!

MARIA
Madam, there is at the gate a young gentleman much desires to speak with you.

LADY OLIVIA
From the Count Orsino, is it?

MARIA
I know not, madam. 'Tis a fair young man, and well attended.

LADY OLIVIA
Who of my people hold him in delay?

MARIA
Sir Toby, madam, your kinsman.

LADY OLIVIA
Fetch him off, I pray you; he speaks nothing but madman. Fie on him!

EXIT MARIA.

LADY OLIVIA (CONT'D)
You go, Malvolio. If it is a request from the count, say I am sick, or not at home – whatever you like to dismiss him.

LADY OLIVIA
Go you, Malvolio. If it be a suit from the count, I am sick or not at home - what you will*, to dismiss it.

**Note: 'What you will' the alternate title for the play. See the historical notes at the beginning for further explanation.*

EXIT MALVOLIO.

LADY OLIVIA (CONT'D)
(*to Feste*) Now you see, sir, how your fooling grows tiresome, and people dislike it.

FESTE
You have spoken of us fools, madonna, as if your eldest son were a fool whose skull God crammed full of brains! – And here he comes, one of your kin with a most weak head.

LADY OLIVIA
Now you see, sir, how your fooling grows old, and people dislike it.

FESTE
Thou hast spoke for us, madonna, as if thy eldest son should be a fool -whose skull Jove cram with brains! - For here he comes, one of thy kin has a most weak pia mater*.

**Note: 'Pia mater' – a membrane surrounding the brain. He has brains but so little holding them in that his intelligence escapes.*

ENTER A DRUNK SIR TOBY BELCH.

LADY OLIVIA
Upon my honour, half drunk! Who was it at the door, uncle?

LADY OLIVIA
By mine honour, half drunk. What is he at the gate, cousin?

SIR TOBY BELCH
A gentleman.

SIR TOBY BELCH
A gentleman.

LADY OLIVIA
A gentleman? What gentleman?

LADY OLIVIA
A gentleman? What gentleman?

SIR TOBY BELCH
'Tis a gentleman here…

SIR TOBY BELCH
'Tis a gentleman here -

SIR TOBY BELCH INDICATES HIMSELF AND BELCHES LOUDLY.

SIR TOBY BELCH (CONT'D)
A curse on these pickled herrings!

SIR TOBY BELCH
A plague o' these pickle-herring!

FESTE LAUGHS AT THE DRUNKEN DISPLAY BY SIR TOBY.

SIR TOBY BELCH (CONT'D)
(*to Feste*) How are you, drunken fool?

SIR TOBY BELCH
[*To Feste.*] How now, sot?

FESTE
(*still laughing*) Good, sir Toby!

FESTE
Good Sir Toby!

LADY OLIVIA
Uncle, uncle, how have you succumbed to this lethargy so early?

LADY OLIVIA
Cousin, cousin, how have you come so early by this lethargy?

SIR TOBY BELCH
(*mishearing her*) Lechery? I defy lechery! There's someone at the main entrance.

SIR TOBY BELCH
Lechery? I defy lechery! There's one at the gate.

LADY OLIVIA
(*exasperated*) Yes, indeed, who is he?

LADY OLIVIA
Ay, marry, what is he?

SIR TOBY BELCH
Let him be the devil if he wants to be, I don't care – give me faith, I say. Well, it's all the same.

SIR TOBY BELCH
Let him be the devil and he will, I care not - give me faith, say I. Well, it's all one.

EXIT SIR TOBY BELCH.

LADY OLIVIA SHAKES HER HEAD IN DISBELIEF AS HE STAGGERS OUT.

SHE TURNS AND ADDRESSES FESTE.

LADY OLIVIA
(*to Feste*) What's a drunken man like, fool?

LADY OLIVIA
What's a drunken man like, fool?

FESTE
Like a drowned man, a fool, and a madman. One drink too many makes him a fool, the second makes him mad, and the third drowns him.

FESTE
Like a drowned man, a fool, and a madman. One draught above heat makes him a fool, the second mads him, and a third drowns him.

LADY OLIVIA
Go find the coroner, let him hold an inquest for my uncle, he's in the third stage of drunkenness – he's drowned. Go look after him.

LADY OLIVIA
Go thou and seek the crowner, and let him sit o' my coz; for he's in the third degree of drink, he's drowned. Go look after him.

FESTE
He is only at the mad stage, madonna, and now the fool shall look after the madman.

FESTE
He is but mad yet, madonna, and the fool shall look to the madman.

EXIT FESTE.

RE-ENTER MALVOLIO.

MALVOLIO
Madam, the young fellow at the door swears he must speak with you. I told him you were sick. He tells me he knew this already, but he must speak with you. I then told him you were asleep, he seemed to be aware of this too, but still says he must speak with you. What shall I say to him, my lady? He's prepared against any denial.

MALVOLIO
Madam, yond young fellow swears he will speak with you. I told him you were sick; he takes on him to understand so much, and therefore comes to speak with you. I told him you were asleep; he seems to have a foreknowledge of that too, and therefore comes to speak with you. What is to be said to him, lady? He's fortified against any denial.

LADY OLIVIA
Tell him he shall not speak with me.

LADY OLIVIA
Tell him he shall not speak with me.

MALVOLIO
He's been told this, and he says he'll stand at your door like a flag pole, and be the legs of a bench until he speaks with you.

MALVOLIO
H'as been told so; and he says he'll stand at your door like a sheriff's post, and be the supporter to a bench*, but he'll speak with you.

**Note: 'Sheriff's post' – a pole outside a magistrate's office to mark its location, not, as commonly assumed, a board for notices to be posted.*

'Supporter to a bench' – a bench has legs supporting it which do not move.

LADY OLIVIA
What kind of a man is he?

LADY OLIVIA
What kind o' man is he?

MALVOLIO
Well, one of the human kind.

MALVOLIO
Why, of mankind.

LADY OLIVIA
What type of man?

LADY OLIVIA
What manner of man?

MALVOLIO
A very rude type. He says he will speak with you whether you want to or not.

MALVOLIO
Of very ill manner: he'll speak with you, will you or no.

LADY OLIVIA
(*exasperated*) What does he look like and how old is he?

LADY OLIVIA
Of what personage and years is he?

MALVOLIO
Not yet old enough to be a man, nor young enough to be a boy – like a peapod before it fills with peas, or an apple just before it ripens. Like the turn of the tide, he's between boy and man. He is very fine-looking, and his voice is quite shrill. You'd think he'd only recently stopped being breast fed.

MALVOLIO
Not yet old enough for a man, nor young enough for a boy - as a squash is before 'tis a peascod, or a codling when 'tis almost an apple. 'Tis with him in standing water, between boy and man. He is very well-favoured, and he speaks very shrewishly. One would think his mother's milk were scarce out of him.

LADY OLIVIA
Allow him in. And call in my maid.

LADY OLIVIA
Let him approach. Call in my gentlewoman.

MALVOLIO
(*shouts*) Maid! – My lady calls!

MALVOLIO
Gentlewoman! - my lady calls.

LADY OLIVIA GRIMACES AS MALVOLIO LEAVES.

MARIA HURRIES IN WITH A QUICK CURTSEY.

LADY OLIVIA
(*to Maria*) Give me my veil, quickly, throw it over my face. And once again we'll hear Orsino's pleas.

LADY OLIVIA
Give me my veil; come, throw it o'er my face.
We'll once more hear Orsino's embassy.

MARIA HELPS OLIVIA PLACE A VEIL OVER HER FACE.

ENTER VIOLA (AS CESARIO) WITH ATTENDANTS.

VIOLA LOOKS AROUND AT THE COUNTESS AND HER ATTENDANTS, ALL ELEGANTLY DRESSED LADIES, AND ADDRESSES THEM.

VIOLA (AS CESARIO)
The honourable lady of the house, which one is she?

VIOLA
The honourable lady of the house, which is she?

LADY OLIVIA
Speak to me, I shall answer for her. What is it you wish?

LADY OLIVIA
Speak to me, I shall answer for her. Your will?

VIOLA STARTS HER SPEECH AS IF RECITING SOMETHING MEMORISED.

VIOLA (AS CESARIO)
Most radiant, exquisite, and unmatchable beauty…

VIOLA
Most radiant, exquisite, and unmatchable beauty-

VIOLA PAUSES, SHE NEEDS TO DELIVER THE MESSAGE TO THE COUNTESS IN PERSON. ONCE AGAIN VIOLA ADDRESSES ALL THE LADIES.

VIOLA (AS CESARIO) (CONT'D)
(*to Attendants*) Please tell me if this is the lady of the house, for I've not seen her before. I would hate to waste my speech, especially as it was so excellently well written, and I have taken great pains to memorise it.

VIOLA
I pray you tell me if this be the lady of the house, for I never saw her. I would be loath to cast away my speech; for besides that it is excellently well penned, I have taken great pains to con it.

memorise

THE LADIES GATHERED LAUGH AT VIOLA'S WORDS.

VIOLA (AS CESARIO) (CONT'D)
Good beauties, do not mock me, I am very sensitive to mockery, even when not meant with malice.

VIOLA
Good beauties, let me sustain no scorn; I am very comptible, even to the least sinister usage.

sensitive

LADY OLIVIA
Where have you come from, sir?

LADY OLIVIA
Whence came you, sir?

VIOLA (AS CESARIO)
I can only say what I have memorised in my speech, and the answer to that question was not part of it. Good gentle lady, give me some assurance that you are the lady of the house, so that I may continue with my speech.

VIOLA
I can say little more than I have studied, and that question's out of my part. Good gentle one, give me modest assurance if you be the lady of the house, that I may proceed in my speech.

LADY OLIVIA
Are you a paid actor?

LADY OLIVIA
Are you a comedian?*

**Note: 'Comedian' – an actor, Olivia picks up on the references to scripts and memorising lines. 'Comedy' had a different meaning back in Shakespeare's day, being the style of a play. A person who told jokes was called a clown, or a fool in the case of a paid jester. The three types of play Shakespeare wrote were Comedies, Tragedies, and Histories. Comedies typically had a happy ending, Tragedies had a tragic end, and Histories were adapted from historical events, albeit with more than a little artistic licence.*

VIOLA (AS CESARIO)
No, my dearest lady, and yet, on pain of ridicule I swear, I am not who I play the part of. Are you the lady of the house?

VIOLA

double meaning

No, my profound heart; and yet, by the very fangs of malice I swear, I am not that I play*. Are you the lady of the house?

**Note: 'I am not that I play' – a joke for the audience. They know Viola is not a man, but Olivia does not. The other meaning being that she is acting on behalf of Sir Toby.*

LADY OLIVIA
Unless I falsely claim to be myself, I am.

VIOLA (AS CESARIO)
That's true, if you are her, you are false to yourself, for what is yours to give is not yours to keep to yourself. But this is outside the bounds of my instructions. I will continue with my speech in praise of you, and then come to the heart of the matter.

LADY OLIVIA
If I do not usurp myself, I am.

VIOLA
Most certain, if you are she, you do usurp yourself; for what is yours to bestow* is not yours to reserve. But this is from my commission. I will on with my speech in your praise, and then show you the heart of my message.

**Note: 'Yours to bestow' – double meaning of giving her hand in marriage, and her identity to Viola.*

LADY OLIVIA
Get to the important part, I'll let you skip the praise.

VIOLA (AS CESARIO)
I'm sorry, I took great pains to study it, and it is poetical.

LADY OLIVIA
Then it is more likely to be insincere. I pray you'll keep it to yourself. I heard you were quite rude at my door, I allowed you to meet me to see you rather than hear you. If you are mad, be gone; if you are not, be brief. It is not the right phase of the moon for me to engage in frivolous conversation.

LADY OLIVIA
Come to what is important in't; I forgive you the praise.

VIOLA
Alas, I took great pains to study it, and 'tis poetical.

LADY OLIVIA
It is the more like to be feigned*; I pray you keep it in. I heard you were saucy at my gates, and allowed your approach rather to wonder at you than to hear you. If you be not mad*, be gone; if you have reason, be brief. 'Tis not that time of moon* with me to make one in so skipping a dialogue.

**Note: 'Feigned' – false. Shakespeare often comments on insincere poets and wrote sonnet 130 satirising the over-glorified terms poets use.*

'If you be not mad' – scholars generally agree that this should read 'if you be mad'.

'Time of the moon' – it was believed the lunar cycle contributed to human behaviour, hence the term lunacy.

MARIA TALKS IN NAUTICAL TERMS.

MARIA
(*to Viola*) Will you set sail and leave, sir?

MARIA
Will you hoist sail, sir?

MARIA POINTS TO THE DOOR.

MARIA (CONT'D)
(*pointing*) There lies your passage.

MARIA
Here lies your way.

VIOLA (AS CESARIO)
(*to Maria*) No, dear deckhand, I'll lay anchor here a while longer.
(*to Olivia*) Calm your giant minder, sweet lady.

VIOLA
No, good swabber, I am to hull here a little longer. Some mollification for your giant*, sweet lady.

**Note: 'Giant' – ironic statement, Maria was originally played by a particularly short boy.*

VIOLA (AS CESARIO) (CONT'D)
Tell me what you think, I am a messenger.

VIOLA
Tell me your mind, I am a messenger.*

**Note: This phrase is often given in two parts in modern editions, the first part spoken by Olivia (tell me your mind), the second (I am a messenger) as a reply from Viola. The original texts have Viola speak both parts of the phrase. The later change is because Viola is asking for Olivia's thoughts about her plea so she can report back before she has made her plea.*

LADY OLIVIA
It seems your message is of a hideous nature, judging by the reluctance you have in delivering it. Say what you were sent to say.

VIOLA (AS CESARIO)
It is for your ears only. I bring no declaration of war, and no tax demand, I hold the olive branch in my hand. My words are as full of peace as they are of importance.

LADY OLIVIA
Sure you have some hideous matter to deliver, when the courtesy of it is so fearful. Speak your office.

VIOLA
It alone concerns your ear. I bring no overture of war, no taxation of homage. I hold the olive* in my hand; my words are as full of peace as matter.

**Note: 'Olive' – the olive branch is a symbol of peace.*

LADY OLIVIA
Yet you began rudely. Who are you? What do you want?

VIOLA (AS CESARIO)
The rudeness that came from me was in response to the rudeness I received upon arrival. Who I am and what I want, is as sacred as your virginity – to your ears, divine, to disclose to any other ears would be profanity.

LADY OLIVIA
Yet you began rudely. What are you? What would you?

VIOLA
The rudeness that hath appeared in me have I learned from my entertainment. What I am, and what I would, are as secret as maidenhead: to your ears, divinity*; to any other's, profanation*.

**Note: 'Divinity – profanation' – religious terms, one pure, one impure. Lady Olivia picks up on the divine message and now will twist the message to be of religious meaning.*

LADY OLIVIA ADDRESSES HER ATTENDANTS.

LADY OLIVIA
Leave us alone. I will hear this divine message.

LADY OLIVIA
Give us the place alone; we will hear this divinity*.

**Note: 'Divinity' – religious and also confirming to all she is still a virgin.*

EXIT MARIA AND ALL ATTENDANTS.

LADY OLIVIA (CONT'D) Now, sir, deliver your sermon.	LADY OLIVIA Now, sir, what is your text?
VIOLA (AS CESARIO) Most sweet lady...	VIOLA Most sweet lady -
LADY OLIVIA (*interrupting*) A comforting start, and much may be said in its favour. But where does this sermon come from?	LADY OLIVIA A comfortable doctrine*, and much may be said of it. Where lies your text?

**Note: 'Comfortable doctrine' – religious words of comfort.*

VIOLA (AS CESARIO) From the bosom of Orsino.	VIOLA In Orsino's bosom.
LADY OLIVIA From his bosom? In what chapter and verse of his bosom?	LADY OLIVIA In his bosom? In what chapter* of his bosom?

**Note: 'Chapter' – religious sermons are quoted from chapters and verses in the Bible.*

VIOLA (AS CESARIO) To answer by this method – from the first chapter of his heart.	VIOLA To answer by the method, in the first of his heart.
LADY OLIVIA Oh, I have read it, it is false doctrine. Have you no more to say?	LADY OLIVIA O, I have read it, it is heresy. Have you no more to say?
VIOLA (AS CESARIO) Good madam, let me see your face.	VIOLA Good madam, let me see your face.
LADY OLIVIA Have you any orders from your master to negotiate with my face? You've now gone astray from your sermon, but I'll open the curtain and show you the picture.	LADY OLIVIA Have you any commission from your lord to negotiate with my face? You are now out of your text; but we will draw the curtain and show you the picture.

**Note: 'Curtain' – pictures were kept behind curtains to protect them from dust, damage and sunlight.*

LADY OLIVIA UNVEILS.
THEY NOW TALK AS IF OLIVIA'S FACE IS A PAINTING.

LADY OLIVIA (CONT'D)
Look at me, sir, just the same as I was before. Isn't it well made?

VIOLA (AS CESARIO)
Excellently made…

LADY OLIVIA
Look you, sir, such a one I was this present. Is't not well done?

VIOLA
Excellently done,

VIOLA PAUSES AS SHE EXAMINES OLIVIA'S FACE.

VIOLA (AS CESARIO)
… if it's all God's work.

LADY OLIVIA
It won't fade, sir, it will endure wind and rain.

VIOLA
if God did all.

LADY OLIVIA
'Tis in grain*, sir; 'twill endure wind and weather.

**Note: 'In grain' – colourfast/permanent colouring, for clothing dyes and paint. (ingrained)*

VIOLA (AS CESARIO)
It is beauty honestly mixed, the reds and whites being painted on by nature's sweet and artful hand. Lady, you are the cruellest woman alive if you go to the grave leaving the world no copy of your beauty.

VIOLA
'Tis beauty truly blent, whose red and white
Nature's own sweet and cunning hand laid on.
Lady, you are the cruell'st she alive
If you will lead these graces to the grave,
And leave the world no copy*.

**Note: 'Leave no copy' – Shakespeare often uses this description for unmarried, young women, meaning that if they do not marry, and therefore produce no children, they will not pass on their beauty, it will end when they die.*

In the next speech Olivia breaks the rhythm by speaking in prose, twisting the meaning of the word 'copy' to mean a written list .It then reverts back to blank verse.

LADY OLIVIA
Oh, sir, I will not be so hard-hearted. I will hand out lists detailing my beauty. They will itemise every component part described to my liking, like so: Item - two lips moderately red. Item - two grey eyes, with accompanying lids. Item - one neck, one chin, and so forth.
Were you sent here to audit me?

VIOLA (AS CESARIO)
I can see what you are – you are too vain. But you are beautiful, even if you are the devil.
My lord and master is in love with you. Oh, such great love that could only be matched by your unmatched beauty.

LADY OLIVIA
O, sir, I will not be so hard-hearted; I will give out divers schedules of my beauty. It shall be inventoried, and every particle and utensil labelled to my will, as: item, two lips indifferent red; item, two grey eyes, with lids to them; item, one neck, one chin, and so forth. Were you sent hither to praise me?

VIOLA
I see you what you are - you are too proud*;
But if you were the devil, you are fair.
My lord and master loves you. O, such love
Could be but recompensed though you were crowned
The nonpareil of beauty.

**Note: 'Proud' – the devil was beautiful and banished from heaven for being proud/vain.*

LADY OLIVIA
How does he love me?

LADY OLIVIA
How does he love me?

VIOLA (AS CESARIO)
With an adoring love, with floods of tears, with thundering groans and fiery sighs.

VIOLA
With adorations, fertile tears,
With groans that thunder love, with sighs of fire.

LADY OLIVIA
Your master knows the way I feel - I cannot love him. But I accept he is virtuous, I know he is noble, of good wealth, full of the vigours of youth, spoken of in high praise, open minded, educated, brave, in good physical shape, and a well-mannered person, but despite all this I cannot love him. He should have come to accept this answer long ago.

LADY OLIVIA
Your lord does know my mind; I cannot love him.
Yet I suppose him virtuous, know him noble,
Of great estate, of fresh and stainless youth;
In voices well divulged, free, learned, and valiant,
And in dimension and the shape of nature
A gracious person; but yet I cannot love him.
He might have took his answer long ago.

VIOLA (AS CESARIO)
If I loved you with the fire my master holds for you, suffering such misery in life due to your denial of love, I too would not understand nor find any sense in your answer.

VIOLA
If I did love you in my master's flame,
With such a suff'ring, such a deadly life,
In your denial I would find no sense;
I would not understand it

LADY OLIVIA
Why, what would you do if you loved me?

LADY OLIVIA
Why, what would you?*

**Note: Lady Olivia seems to be quite taken with the young man she sees.*

VIOLA (AS CESARIO)
Build a wooden hut in front of your gate and call daily upon my love inside the house. I'd write devoted songs of unrequited love and sing them loud even in the dead of night. I'd shout your name to the echoing hills, and make the nymph Echo call back "Olivia!" Oh, you would not be able to live on this earth and not feel pity for me.

VIOLA
Make me a willow cabin at your gate,
And call upon my soul within the house;
Write loyal cantons of contemned love,
And sing them loud even in the dead of night;
Halloo your name to the reverberate hills,
And make the babbling gossip* of the air
Cry out "Olivia!" O, you should not rest
Between the elements of air and earth
But you should pity me.

**Note: 'Babbling gossip' – referring to Echo, the nymph from Greek mythology. Zeus would visit the nymphs until his wife Hera caught him with the nymph Echo who lied on behalf of Zeus. Enraged, Hera made Echo capable of only repeating the last words spoken to her. As a result of this, Echo was unable to tell Narcissus she loved him and instead watched him slowly fall in love with himself.*

LADY OLIVIA
You may just succeed. What is your status?

LADY OLIVIA
You might do much.
What is your parentage?

VIOLA (AS CESARIO)
Above my station, yet in a good state, I am a gentleman.

VIOLA
Above my fortunes*, yet my state* is well.
I am a gentleman.

**Note: 'Fortunes' – play on the word's meaning of both wealth and luck.*

LADY OLIVIA
Go back to your master. I cannot love him. Tell him to send no more messengers, unless, perchance, you return to me to tell me his reaction. Farewell, I thank you for your efforts. Take this money.

LADY OLIVIA
Get you to your lord.
I cannot love him. Let him send no more,
Unless, perchance, you come to me again
To tell me how he takes it. Fare you well.
I thank you for your pains. Spend this for me.

LADY OLIVIA OFFERS VIOLA MONEY.

VIOLA (AS CESARIO)
I require no tip, lady, keep your money. It is my master, not myself, that lacks recompense. May Cupid turn the man you love's heart to stone.
And then let your love, like my master's, be
Firmly rejected! Farewell, cruel beauty.

VIOLA
I am no fee'd post, lady; keep your purse;
My master, not myself, lacks recompense.
Love make his heart of flint that you shall love,
And let your fervour, like my master's, be
Placed in contempt! Farewell, fair cruelty. *

EXIT VIOLA.

**Note: Note the rhyming couplet as Viola leaves the stage.*

LADY OLIVIA
(*aside*) "What is your status?"
"Above my station, yet in a good state. I am a gentleman."
I am sure you are. Your tongue, your face, your limbs, your actions and spirit show you are a gentleman of the highest degree. – Wait! - Not so fast…

LADY OLIVIA
"What is your parentage?"
"Above my fortunes, yet my state is well.
I am a gentleman." I'll be sworn thou art.
Thy tongue, thy face, thy limbs, actions, and spirit,
Do give thee fivefold blazon. Not too fast! - soft, soft;

**Note: 'Fivefold blazon' – a coat of arms, therefore a confirmed gentleman.*

LADY OLIVIA PAUSES AT A SUDDEN THOUGHT.

LADY OLIVIA (CONT'D)
(*aside*) Unless the man were like the master. What then? Can one catch the disease so quickly? I think this youth's fine qualities are creeping into my eyes subtly by stealth. Well, then let it do so.
(*calls*) Malvolio, come here!

LADY OLIVIA
Unless the master were the man. How now?
Even so quickly may one catch the plague?
Methinks I feel this youth's perfections
With an invisible and subtle stealth
To creep in at mine eyes. Well, let it be.
What ho, Malvolio!

RE-ENTER MALVOLIO HURRIEDLY.

MALVOLIO At your service, madam.	MALVOLIO Here, madam, at your service.
LADY OLIVIA Run after that obstinate messenger who just left, the Count's man. He left this ring behind.	LADY OLIVIA Run after that same peevish messenger, The County's man. He left this ring behind him,

SHE TAKES A RING FROM HER FINGER AND HANDS IT TO MALVOLIO.

LADY OLIVIA (CONT'D) Whether I want it or not, tell him I'll not have it. Tell him not to encourage his master, nor give him any hope – I am not interested in him. Should the youth come back tomorrow I'll let him know my reasons. Now hurry, Malvolio.	LADY OLIVIA Would I or not. Tell him I'll none of it. Desire him not to flatter with his lord, Nor hold him up with hopes: I am not for him. If that the youth will come this way tomorrow, I'll give him reasons for't. Hie thee, Malvolio.
MALVOLIO I will, madam.	MALVOLIO Madam, I will.

EXIT MALVOLIO IN A STATELY MANNER WITH NO RUSH.

LADY OLIVIA (*aside*) I don't know what I'm doing, and I fear my eye is leading my mind astray. *Fate show your hand. It is not up to us.* *What will be, will be, and let it be thus!*	LADY OLIVIA I do I know not what, and fear to find Mine eye too great a flatterer for my mind. *Fate, show thy force. Ourselves we do not owe*;* *What is decreed must be -and be this so!*

**Note: 'Owe' – own. Originally shortened from 'owen'.*

EXIT LADY OLIVIA.

ACT II

ILLYRIA

THE SEA COAST AND OLIVIA'S HOUSE

"SOME ARE BORN GREAT, SOME ACHIEVE GREATNESS, AND SOME HAVE GREATNESS THRUST UPON 'EM."

ACT II

ACT II SCENE I

A SEA COAST OF ILLYRIA.

ANTONIO, A SEA CAPTAIN, AND SEBASTIAN - WHO IS THE TWIN BROTHER OF VIOLA - HAVE LANDED ON A SHORE.

Note: Antonio had rescued Sebastian three months earlier and cared for him since..

Except for Antonio's last speech this scene is written in prose.

ANTONIO
You won't stay with me any longer? Do you want me to go with you?

SEBASTIAN
Thank you, but no. The stars are not in my favour, the ominous outlook of my fate may infect yours. So I politely ask that you leave me to bear my troubles alone. It would be poor repayment for the kindness you have shown to lay any of them on you.

ANTONIO
At least let me know where you are headed.

SEBASTIAN
No, really, sir, I have no fixed plans, and no purpose. But I see in you a refined politeness that keeps you from prying further, therefore, Antonio, as we are parting I feel it only good manners to let you know a little about me. I can let you know this much, my real name is Sebastian, not, as I had called myself, Roderigo. My father was Sebastian of Messaline whom I know you have heard of. He raised myself and my sister, both born within an hour of each other, and if the heavens had allowed, would have ended our lives the same way! But you sir, changed that, because an hour before you rescued me from the waves of the sea my sister was drowned.

ANTONIO
Will you stay no longer? Nor will you not that I go with you?

SEBASTIAN
By your patience, no. My stars shine darkly over me; the malignancy of my fate might perhaps distemper yours; therefore I shall crave of you your leave, that I may bear my evils alone. It were a bad recompense for your love to lay any of them on you.

ANTONIO
Let me yet know of you whither you are bound.

SEBASTIAN
No, sooth, sir; my determinate voyage is mere extravagancy. But I perceive in you so excellent a touch of modesty that you will not extort from me what I am willing to keep in; therefore it charges me in manners the rather to express myself. You must know of me then, Antonio, my name is Sebastian, which I called Roderigo. My father was that Sebastian of Messaline whom I know you have heard of. He left behind him myself and a sister, both born in an hour - if the heavens had been pleased, would we had so ended! But you, sir, altered that, for some hour before you took me from the breach of the sea was my sister drowned.

ANTONIO
Terrible news!

SEBASTIAN
A lady, sir, who though it was said much resembled me, was also renowned for her beauty. Though it would be over-stretching my imagination to believe that, I will go as far as to say she bore a mind that even envy would agree was beautiful.

ANTONIO
Alas the day!

SEBASTIAN
A lady, sir, though it was said she much resembled me, was yet of many accounted beautiful; but though I could not with such estimable wonder overfar believe that, yet thus far I will boldly publish her: she bore a mind that envy could not but call fair.

SEBASTIAN WEEPS, SALTY TEARS STREAMING DOWN HIS FACE.

SEBASTIAN (CONT'D)
She is drowned now, sir, with salt water, though I seem to drown her memory with even more.

ANTONIO
Forgive me, sir, for not being more hospitable.

SEBASTIAN
Oh, good Antonio, forgive me for the trouble I have put you to.

ANTONIO
Save me from dying out of pity for you, let me be your servant.

SEBASTIAN
Unless you wish to undo the good you have done by killing the one you rescued, do not ask this. I must leave. My heart is full of your kindness, and I am so close to the behaviour of my mother that at the least opportunity my eyes again will show how I really feel. I am heading to the court of Count Orsino. Farewell.

SEBASTIAN
She is drowned already, sir, with salt water, though I seem to drown her remembrance again with more.

ANTONIO
Pardon me, sir, your bad entertainment.

SEBASTIAN
O good Antonio, forgive me your trouble.

ANTONIO
If you will not murder me for my love, let me be your servant.

SEBASTIAN
If you will not undo what you have done, that is, kill him whom you have recovered, desire it not. Fare ye well at once. My bosom is full of kindness, and I am yet so near the manners of my mother that upon the least occasion more mine eyes will tell tales of me. I am bound to the Count Orsino's court. Farewell.

EXIT SEBASTIAN. ANTONIO CALLS OUT AFTER HIM.

ANTONIO
The kindness of all the gods go with you! I have many enemies in Orsino's court or I would see you there shortly. (*he pauses in thought*)
But come what may my love for you's so strong,
The danger will seem fun, I'll go along.

ANTONIO
The gentleness of all the gods go with thee!
I have many enemies in Orsino's court,
Else would I very shortly see thee there.
But come what may, I do adore thee so,
That danger shall seem sport, and I will go.

ANTONIO EXITS, FOLLOWING SEBASTIAN.

ACT II SCENE II

A STREET NEAR OLIVIA'S HOUSE.

ENTER VIOLA (AS CESARIO) WALKING AT A LEISURELY PACE.
MALVOLIO HURRIES BEHIND HER, CARRYING A RING.

MALVOLIO CATCHES UP TO VIOLA.

MALVOLIO (*breathless*) Were you just now visiting the Countess Olivia?	MALVOLIO Were not you ev'n now with the Countess Olivia?
VIOLA (AS CESARIO) Just now, sir. The time it takes to walk at a leisurely pace to this point.	VIOLA Even now, sir; on a moderate pace I have since arrived but hither.
MALVOLIO She returns this ring to you, sir.	MALVOLIO She returns this ring to you, sir.

MALVOLIO PRODUCES THE RING. CONFUSED, VIOLA DOES NOT TAKE IT.
SHE KNOWS NOTHING ABOUT THE RING.

MALVOLIO (CONT'D) (*grumpy and aloof*) You might have saved me my pains had you taken it away yourself. In addition, she adds that you should make it very clear to your master that she'll have nothing to do with him. And one more thing, that you never be so bold as to come again on his behalf, unless it is to report on your master's reaction to this message.	MALVOLIO You might have saved me my pains, to have taken it away yourself. She adds, moreover, that you should put your lord into a desperate assurance she will none of him. And one thing more, that you be never so hardy to come again in his affairs, unless it be to report your lord's taking of this. Receive it so

MALVOLIO OFFERS VIOLA THE RING AGAIN.

MALVOLIO (CONT'D) Here, take it.	MALVOLIO Receive it so

WHEN VIOLA HESITATES MALVOLIO THROWS THE RING ON THE GROUND.
VIOLA, THINKING QUICKLY, TRIES TO TWIST THE SITUATION.

VIOLA (AS CESARIO) She took the ring from me, I no longer want it.	VIOLA She took the ring of me; I'll none of it.

MALVOLIO
Come, sir, you rudely threw it to her, and her wish is that it should be returned in like manner. If it is worth stooping down for, there it lies in your sight. If not, let it be his that finds it.

MALVOLIO
Come, sir, you peevishly threw it to her; and her will is it should be so returned. If it be worth stooping for, there it lies in your eye; if not, be it his that finds it.

EXIT MALVOLIO, NOSE IN THE AIR

VIOLA (AS CESARIO)
(*aside*) I didn't leave a ring with her. What does the lady mean? Heaven forbid that my appearance has charmed her! She looked me over a lot, in fact, so much so that I thought her eyes had tied up her tongue because she spoke in fits and starts as if distracted. She loves me that's for sure. It's the cunning of her passion which invites me back by sending this rude messenger.
She won't have my master's ring! Ha! He didn't send her one. I am the man she's after. If that is true, poor lady, she may as well be in love with a dream. I see my disguise is a wickedness in which the devil is at work. How easy it is for handsome deceivers to use their looks to soften women's hearts! Alas, our femininity is the fault, not us, how we were made is how we are. How will this all end? My master loves her dearly, and I, a pathetic mixture of sexes, am as fond of him as he is of her, and she, mistakenly seems to dote on me. What will become of all this? As a man I cannot pursue my master's love, and as a woman I – regrettably – cause poor Olivia wasted sighs for me!
Oh, time you must untangle this, not I.
For it's a knot that I cannot untie.

VIOLA
I left no ring with her: what means this lady?
Fortune forbid my outside have not charmed her!
She made good view of me; indeed, so much
That methought her eyes had lost her tongue,
For she did speak in starts distractedly.
She loves me sure; the cunning of her passion
Invites me in this churlish messenger.
None of my lord's ring! Why, he sent her none.
I am the man. If it be so, as 'tis,
Poor lady, she were better love a dream.
Disguise, I see thou art a wickedness
Wherein the pregnant enemy does much.
How easy is it for the proper false
In women's waxen hearts to set their forms!
Alas, our frailty is the cause, not we,
For such as we are made of, such we be.
How will this fadge?* My master loves her dearly,
And I, poor monster, fond as much on him,
And she, mistaken, seems to dote on me.
What will become of this? As I am man,
My state is desperate for my master's love;
As I am woman - now alas the day! -
What thriftless sighs shall poor Olivia breathe!
O time, thou must untangle this, not I;
It is too hard a knot for me t'untie.

**Note: 'Fadge' – turn out, result of.*

Asides were often spoken directly to the audience in this play. It is up to individual directors how they wish to handle the asides, there is no hard fast rule.

VIOLA (AS CESARIO) PICKS UP THE RING AND EXITS.

ACT II SCENE III

A ROOM IN OLIVIA'S HOUSE, VERY LATE AT NIGHT.

ENTER SIR TOBY BELCH CARRYING A CANDLE AND A TANKARD.

HE DRUNKENLY BECKONS TO SIR ANDREW WHO LAGS BEHIND.

SIR TOBY BELCH Come on, Sir Andrew.	SIR TOBY BELCH Approach, Sir Andrew.

ENTER A DRUNKEN SIR ANDREW AGUECHEEK.

SIR TOBY BELCH (CONT'D) To be out of bed after midnight is to be up early. And to arise early in the morning – you know the saying – *diluculo sugere*.	SIR TOBY BELCH Not to be abed after midnight is to be up betimes; and 'diluculo surgere'* thou know'st

**Note: 'Diluculo sugere' – To arise at down. Every schoolboy back then would be familiar with the Latin saying, which concludes 'is the most wholesome thing in the world'.*

Obviously from what follows, Sir Andrew is not familiar with the saying suggesting he was not well educated for the time.

SIR ANDREW AGUECHEEK No, I swear, I don't know it, but I know that to be up late is to be up late.	SIR ANDREW AGUECHEEK Nay, by my troth, I know not; but I know to be up late is to be up late.
SIR TOBY BELCH Your logic is faulty. I hate it as much as an empty tankard.	SIR TOBY BELCH A false conclusion; I hate it as an unfilled can.

SIR TOBY SADLY TIPS HIS TANKARD UPSIDE DOWN TO SHOW IT IS EMPTY.

SIR TOBY BELCH (CONT'D) To be up after midnight not having gone to bed is early. So, to go to bed after midnight is to go to bed early. Don't our lives consist of the four elements?	SIR TOBY BELCH To be up after midnight and to go to bed then, is early; so that to go to bed after midnight is to go to bed betimes. Does not our lives consist of the four elements?

**Note: 'Four elements' – it was believed the body was made up from the four basic elements - earth, water, air and fire.*

SIR ANDREW AGUECHEEK Indeed, so they say, but I think it actually consists of eating and drinking.	SIR ANDREW AGUECHEEK Faith, so they say; but I think it rather consists of eating and drinking.

SIR TOBY BELCH You are a scholar, sir. In that case let us eat and drink. (*calls*) Marian! I say! A flagon of wine!	SIR TOBY BELCH Th'art a scholar; let us therefore eat and drink. Marian*, I say, a stoup* of wine!

**Note: 'Marian' – Her name is listed as Maria, she calls herself Mary, and he now calls her Marian, possibly his drunkenness.*

'Stoup' – A large tankard, typically two pints (just over 1 litre) in volume.

ENTER FESTE THE FOOL.

SIR ANDREW AGUECHEEK Here comes the fool, instead.	SIR ANDREW AGUECHEEK Here comes the fool, i'faith.
FESTE How are you, my hearties? Did you ever see the picture 'We Three Loggerheads'?	FESTE How now, my hearts? Did you never see the picture of We Three?*

We Three Loggerheads

**Note: 'We Three' – referring to a comic painting, a famous version of which is shown on the left; 'Wee Three Logerheads' consisting of two fools. It could be found hanging in pubs or used as inn signs and would have been well known to the audience.*

The confusing title of 'We Three' made sense when the viewer of the picture realised that the third fool was themself. Feste suggests the two are fools just like him, making three.

The two fools on the left were Tom Derry, court jester to James I of England, and Muckle John, thought to have been from the court of Charles I. This was not the actual painting referred to as this play was written in 1601 before James or Charles came to the throne in England.

Earlier versions of the picture existed which showed two asses heads which may explain Sir Toby's reply 'Welcome, ass' making this an early 'meme' with various versions in existence. Modern versions can still be found with two asses and the words "When shall we three meet again", and as a pub sign as shown to the right.

English Pub Sign

SIR TOBY BELCH Welcome, ass. Now sing us a round.	SIR TOBY BELCH Welcome, ass. Now let's have a catch*.

**Note: 'Catch' – a round, a popular type of song in Shakespeare's time with identical overlapping parts requiring three voices.*

SIR ANDREW AGUECHEEK
Upon my word, the fool has an excellent voice. I'd give forty shillings to be so fine a dancer, and so sweet a singer as the fool is.
(*to Feste*) In all truth, you were in fine fooling last night when you spoke of Pigrogromitus of the Vapians passing the equinoctial of Queubus. It was very good indeed. I sent sixpence for your dalliance – did you get it?

SIR ANDREW AGUECHEEK
By my troth, the fool has an excellent breast. I had rather than forty shillings I had such a leg, and so sweet a breath to sing, as the fool has. In sooth, thou wast in very gracious fooling last night, when thou spok'st of Pigrogromitus, of the Vapians passing the equinoctial* of Queubus;* 'twas very good, i'faith. I sent thee sixpence for thy leman* - hadst it?

**Note: 'Equinoctial' – the equator in the heavens, a projection into space of the Earth's equator. The whole phrase is pseudo astrological nonsense, made up but sounding learned. Queubus probably refers to Phoebus (Apollo) whose chariot crosses the equator at the equinox*

'Leman' – an illicit lover or dalliance..

FESTE
I secreted your *small* gratuity in my clothing. As Malvolio's nose is bent, and my lady is upper class, a cheap ale house would not be sufficient.

FESTE
I did impeticos* thy gratillity*; for Malvolio's nose is no whipstock, my lady has a white hand*, and the Myrmidons* are no bottle-ale houses.

**Note: 'Impeticos' – from burlesque dancers placing tips in their petticoats.*

'Gratillity' – another word with burlesque roots meaning a small gratuity.

'Whipstock' – whip handle – Malvolio's nose is not straight, a derogatory term.

'White hand' – upper class ladies were renowned for their white skin to show off that they never had to do a day's work.

'Myrmidons' – expensive place to take a lover. Named after the personal troops of Achilles

- Feste jokes that Olivia and Malvolio are his illicit lovers and would be insulted at the small amount as they would need to be taken somewhere expensive, not a cheap ale house.

SIR ANDREW AGUECHEEK
(*laughing*) Excellent! Why, this is fooling at its finest, when all is said and done. Now sing a song.

SIR ANDREW AGUECHEEK
Excellent! Why, this is the best fooling, when all is done. Now a song.

SIR TOBY OFFERS A SMALL SILVER COIN TO FESTE FROM A HANDFUL OF COINS.

SIR TOBY BELCH
Come on, here's sixpence for you. Let's have a song.

SIR TOBY BELCH
Come on, there is sixpence for you. Let's have a song.

SIR ANDREW TAKES A COIN FROM SIR TOBY'S HAND WITHOUT ASKING.

SIR ANDREW AGUECHEEK
There's a tanner* from me too. If one knight gives a...

SIR ANDREW AGUECHEEK
There's a testril* of me too. If one knight give a -

**Note: 'Testril' – another coin worth sixpence, originally a shilling coin called a teston which was devalued to be worth sixpence.*

A 'Tanner' was a much used term for a sixpence coin up until the introduction of decimal currency in England in 1971. It was worth 2.5p in the new decimal coinage. Originally there were twelve pennies in a shilling, and 20 shillings in a pound which made for harder maths when spending and giving change. The new system made it 100 new pennies in a pound instead of 240 old pennies which had been in use since Roman occupation times.

FESTE
(*pocketing the coins*) Would you prefer a love song or a song about living the good times?

FESTE
Would you have a love-song, or a song of good life*?

**Note: 'Good life' – living it up, a revelling song, but Sir Andrew takes the term literally below.*

SIR TOBY BELCH
A love song, a love song.

SIR ANDREW AGUECHEEK
Yes, yes, I don't care for good living.

SIR TOBY BELCH
A love-song, a love-song.

SIR ANDREW AGUECHEEK
Ay, ay; I care not for good life.

THE CLOWN SINGS, AND PLAYS HIS TABOR BETWEEN VERSES.

FESTE
(sings)
Oh, mistress mine, where are you roaming?
Oh, stay and hear, your true love's coming,
He can sing both high and low.
Traipse no further, pretty sweeting,
Journeys end in lovers meeting,
Every foolish son does know.

FESTE
[sings]
O mistress mine, where are you roaming?
O, stay and hear, your true-love's coming,
That can sing both high and low.
*Trip no further, pretty sweeting;**
Journeys end in lovers meeting,
Every wise man's son doth know.*

**Note: 'Sweeting' – common term then for sweetheart.*

'Wise man's son' – a fool. From an old proverb 'A wise man commonly has foolish children'.

SIR ANDREW AGUECHEEK
(*over the pipe playing*) Very good indeed.

SIR TOBY BELCH
Good, good.

SIR ANDREW AGUECHEEK
Excellent good, i'faith.

SIR TOBY BELCH
Good, good.

FESTE CONTINUES HIS SONG.

Tabor pipe

FESTE	FESTE
(sings) *What is love? Not for the future,* *Current joy gives current laughter,* *What's to come is still unsure.* *By holding back there won't be plenty,* *So kiss me now, sweet young and twenty,* *Youth's a state that won't endure.*	*[Sings.]* *What is love? 'Tis not hereafter;* *Present mirth hath present laughter;* *What's to come is still unsure.* *In delay there lies no plenty;* *Then come kiss me, sweet and twenty*,* *Youth's a stuff will not endure.*

**Note: 'Sweet and twenty' has two possible meanings, sweet twenty-year old, or sweet twenty times over. As the line which follows mentions youth it suggests twenty-years of age.*

SIR ANDREW AGUECHEEK	SIR ANDREW AGUECHEEK
A mellifluous* voice, as true as I am a knight.	A mellifluous* voice, as I am true knight.

**Note: 'Mellifluous' – pleasingly smooth and musical to hear, said pretentiously.*

SIR TOBY BELCH	SIR TOBY BELCH
A contagious breath.	A contagious breath*.

**Note: 'Contagious breath' – play on words, likely to spread emotion or disease.*

SIR ANDREW AGUECHEEK	SIR ANDREW AGUECHEEK
Very sweet and contagious, indeed.	Very sweet and contagious, i'faith.
SIR TOBY BELCH	SIR TOBY BELCH
When you hear using the nose, it is dulcet in contagion. But shall we do the heavenly dance? Shall we rouse the night owl with a song that could drag three souls from one weaver? Shall we do that?	To hear by the nose*, it is dulcet* in contagion. But shall we make the welkin* dance indeed? Shall we rouse the night-owl in a catch that will draw three souls out of one weaver*? Shall we do that?

**Note: 'Hear by the nose' – playing on the word 'breath' earlier.*

'Dulcet' – sweet and soothing.

'Welkin' – the sky or the heavens. Welkin dance is to dance till the sky seems to spin around.

'Three souls' – Music was said to drag the soul from men's bodies, and weavers were famed for singing to keep a rhythm as they worked. They plan raucous singing and dancing.

SIR ANDREW AGUECHEEK	SIR ANDREW AGUECHEEK
If you are a good friend, let's do it. I'm the top dog when it comes to a catchy song.	And you love me, let's do't. I am dog* at a catch.

**Note: 'Dog' – the best.*

FESTE	FESTE
By heavens, sir, and some dogs do catch well.	Byrlady, sir, and some dogs will catch well.

SIR ANDREW AGUECHEEK
Certainly. Let our catchy song be '*You Knave*'.

SIR ANDREW AGUECHEEK
Most certain. Let our catch be 'Thou Knave'*.

**Note: 'Thou Knave' – three singers take turns singing 'hold thy peace, thou knave, and I prithee hold thy peace'.*

FESTE
'*Hold your peace, you knave*', knight? I shall be forced to call you knave instead of knight.

FESTE
` *Hold thy peace, thou knave*,' knight? I shall be constrained in't to call thee knave, knight.

SIR ANDREW AGUECHEEK
It won't be the first time I have caused someone to call me knave. Begin, fool.
It begins, [*sings*] "*Hold your peace*".

SIR ANDREW AGUECHEEK
'Tis not the first time I have constrained one to call me knave. Begin, fool. It begins "*Hold thy peace*".

FESTE
I will never begin if I hold my peace.

FESTE
I shall never begin if I hold my peace.*

**Note: 'Hold my peace' – a deliberate innuendo punning on the word peace/piece.*

SIR ANDREW AGUECHEEK
(*missing the joke*) Very good. Come on, begin.

SIR ANDREW AGUECHEEK
Good, i'faith. Come, begin.

THEY SING A CATCH (A ROUND), ALL MAKING A MERRY RACKET.

MARIA ENTERS NONE TOO HAPPY.

MARIA
What a racket you're all making! If my lady has not woken her steward Malvolio to throw you out the door, never believe me again.

MARIA
What a caterwauling do you keep here! If my lady have not called up her steward Malvolio and bid him turn you out of doors, never trust me.

SIR TOBY BELCH
My lady's a wealthy harridan, we are crafty schemers, Malvolio is Peg the whore, and...
(sings loudly) "Three merry men are we".
Am I not consanguineous? Am I not of her blood? Fiddle-diddle, (*sarcastic*) Lady!
(sings) "There lived a man in Babylon, Lady, Lady."

SIR TOBY BELCH
My lady's a Cataian*, we are politicians, Malvolio's a Peg-a-Ramsey*, and...
[Sings.] "Three merry men be we".
Am not I consanguineous*? Am I not of her blood? Tilly-vally*, Lady.
*[Sings.] "There dwelt a man in Babylon, Lady, Lady."**

**Note: 'Cataian' – Chinese, (Cathay, old name for China) famed for wealth and strict ruling*

'Peg-a-Ramsey' – A popular ribald song about a lady of loose morals called Peg.

'Consanguineous' – people descended from the same ancestor, and difficult to say drunk.

'There dwelt a man...' – Popular song of the time, used for the repetition of 'lady'

FESTE
I'll be damned, admirable fooling by the knight!

FESTE
Beshrew me, the knight's in admirable fooling.

SIR ANDREW AGUECHEEK
Yes, he does well if he's in the mood, and so do I too. He does it more gracefully, but I do it more naturally.

SIR ANDREW AGUECHEEK
Ay, he does well enough if he be disposed, and so do I too. He does it with a better grace, but I do it more natural*.

**Note: 'Natural' also meant an idiot. He inadvertently says he is a natural idiot.*

SIR TOBY BELCH
(sings loudly) "On the twelfth day of December"...

SIR TOBY BELCH
*[Sings.]"O' the twelfth day of December" - **

MARIA
For the love of God, shut up!

MARIA
For the love o'God, peace!

ENTER MALVOLIO IN HIS NIGHTGOWN CARRYING A CANDLE.

MALVOLIO
My masters, are you mad or what? Have you no sense, no manners, no decency, but to gibber away like mischievous children at this time of night? Do you treat my lady's house as an alehouse, where you can shriek out your working men's songs with no consideration of the loudness? Is there no respect of the place, the people, or the time with you?

MALVOLIO
My masters, are you mad? Or what are you? Have you no wit, manners, nor honesty, but to gabble like tinkers at this time of night? Do ye make an alehouse of my lady's house, that ye squeak out your coziers' catches without any mitigation or remorse of voice? Is there no respect of place, persons, nor time in you?

SIR TOBY BELCH
We kept good time in our songs, sir. Go hang yourself!

SIR TOBY BELCH
We did keep time, sir, in our catches. Sneck up!*

**Note: 'Sneck up!' – hung by the neck.*

MALVOLIO
Sir Toby, I must be blunt with you. My lady ordered me to tell you that she provides lodging for you as her relation, though she can in no way relate to your disorderly behaviour. If you can tear yourself away from your misconduct you are welcome to stay at her house, if not, and you'd care to leave her, she'd be very happy to bid you farewell.

MALVOLIO
Sir Toby, I must be round* with you. My lady bade me tell you that though she harbours you as her kinsman, she's nothing allied to your disorders. If you can separate yourself and your misdemeanours you are welcome to the house; if not, and it would please you to take leave of her, she is very willing to bid you farewell.

**Note: 'Round' – plain spoken, punning on the song being a round.*

SIR TOBY BELCH
(sings) "Farewell, dear heart, since I must now be gone."

SIR TOBY BELCH
*[Sings.] "Farewell, dear heart, since I must needs be gone."**

MARIA
(*pleading him to stop*) No, good Sir Toby.

MARIA
Nay, good Sir Toby.

FESTE
(sings second line of song indicating Sir Toby) "His eyes do show his days are almost done."

FESTE
*[Sings.] "His eyes do show his days are almost done."**

**Note: From a popular song of the time (Farewell To Phillis) but with improvised words.*

MALVOLIO
(*wishing it were true*) Is it even possible?

MALVOLIO
Is't even so?

SIR TOBY BELCH
(sings) "But I will never die."

SIR TOBY BELCH
[Sings.] "But I will never die."

FESTE
(sings, points to floor) "Sir Toby, there you lie"

FESTE
[Sings.] "Sir Toby, there you lie."

MALVOLIO
The best place for you.

MALVOLIO
This is much credit to you.

SIR TOBY BELCH
(sings about Malvolio) "Shall I tell him to go?"

SIR TOBY BELCH
[Sings.] "Shall I bid him go?"

FESTE
(sings) "And what if you do?"

FESTE
[Sings.] "What and if you do?"

SIR TOBY BELCH
(sings) "Shall I tell him to go and care not?"

SIR TOBY BELCH
[Sings.] "Shall I bid him go, and spare not?"

FESTE
(sings) "Oh, no, no, no, no, you dare not."

FESTE
[Sings.] "O no, no, no, no, you dare not."*

SIR TOBY BELCH
(*sings*) "*Out of time*".
(*spoken to Feste*) Sir? – *you* lie.

SIR TOBY BELCH
"Out o' *time**", sir? - ye lie*.

**Note: 'Time' – most editions change this to tune - but he did say he kept good time earlier. Feste has broken the rhythm from the original song they parodied by saying an extra 'no'.*

'Ye lie' – This refers to Feste's earlier, 'there you lie'. Sir Toby says it is Feste who is lying.

SIR TOBY BELCH (CONT'D)
(*to Malvolio*) Are you ever not a steward? Do you think that because you are so virtuous there'll be no cake and ale for anyone else?

SIR TOBY BELCH
Art any more than a steward? Dost thou think because thou art virtuous there shall be no more cakes and ale?

FESTE
Yes, by Saint Anne, and spiced wine shall be hot in the mouth too.

FESTE
Yes, by Saint Anne*, and ginger* shall be hot i'th mouth too.

**Note: 'Saint Anne' – mother of the Virgin Mary, an exclamation.*
'Ginger' – used to spice ale or wine and as an aphrodisiac.

SIR TOBY BELCH
(*to Feste*) You are so right.
(*to Malvolio*) Go, sir, and polish your chain with crumbs from the table.
(*to Maria*) A flagon of wine, Maria!

SIR TOBY BELCH
Th'art i'th right. - Go, sir, rub your chain with crumbs.* A stoup of wine, Maria!

**Note: 'Rub your chain with crumbs' – Stewards wore a chain to show their seniority above other servants and would polish them using breadcrumbs.*

MALVOLIO
Mistress Mary, if you value my lady's opinion at any level above contempt, you would not provide the means that cause this disorderly conduct. She'll be informed of this, by my own hand!

MALVOLIO
Mistress Mary, if you prized my lady's favour at anything more than contempt, you would not give means for this uncivil rule. She shall know of it, by this hand.

MALVOLIO SHAKES HIS HAND IN THE AIR AND EXITS.

MARIA CALLS AFTER HIM.

MARIA
Go shake your ears, you ass!

MARIA
Go shake your ears.

SIR ANDREW AGUECHEEK
That's as good as offering a drink to a hungry man. I'll challenge him to a duel, and then not turn up to the fight to make a fool of him.

SIR ANDREW AGUECHEEK
'Twere as good a deed as to drink when a man's ahungry, to challenge him the field, and then to break promise with him and make a fool of him.

SIR TOBY BELCH
Do it, sir knight. I'll write the challenge for you, or deliver your indignation to him verbally.

SIR TOBY BELCH
Do't, knight. I'll write thee a challenge, or I'll deliver thy indignation to him by word of mouth.

MARIA
Sweet Sir Toby, be patient for tonight. Since the count's youthful aide was with my lady today she is now much out of sorts. As for (*sarcastic*) *Monsieur* Malvolio, leave him to me. If I don't goad him into saying foolish things to make him a laughing stock, you can tell me I don't have enough brains to lie down straight in my own bed. I know I can do it.

MARIA
Sweet Sir Toby, be patient for tonight. Since the youth of the count's was today with my lady she is much out of quiet. For Monsieur* Malvolio, let me alone with him; if I do not gull him* into a nayword*, and make him a common recreation, do not think I have wit enough to lie straight in my bed. I know I can do it.

**Note: 'Monsieur' – French word for Mister, mocking Malvolio for his stuck-up attitude.*

'Gull him' – trick him. Gulls were considered stupid birds

'Nayword' – negative word – saying something foolish.

SIR TOBY BELCH
Tell us, tell us. Tell us something about him.

SIR TOBY BELCH
Possess us, possess us; tell us something of him.

MARIA
Goodness me, sir, sometimes he can be so puritanical.

MARIA
Marry, sir, sometimes he is a kind of puritan.

SIR ANDREW AGUECHEEK
Oh, if I thought that I'd beat him like a dog.

SIR ANDREW AGUECHEEK
O, if I thought that I'd beat him like a dog.

SIR TOBY BELCH
What? For being puritanical? Your wonderful reason why, dear knight?

SIR TOBY BELCH
What, for being a puritan? Thy exquisite reason, dear knight?

SIR ANDREW AGUECHEEK
I don't have wonderful reason, but I have good enough reason.

SIR ANDREW AGUECHEEK
I have no exquisite reason for't, but I have reason good enough.

THE TWO MEN LAUGH DRUNKENLY.

MARIA
He's not the devil of a puritan all the time, nor anything else in particular, but he's a grovelling servant for life and a stuck-up ass who learns high and mighty words without understanding their meaning and regurgitates them in great swathes. He has the highest opinion of himself, and truly believes he is so crammed with excellent qualities that everyone looks up to him. And in that inherent weakness I will find ample opportunity to wreak my revenge.

MARIA
The devil a Puritan that he is, or anything constantly but a time-pleaser, an affectioned ass that cons state without book and utters it by great swarths; the best persuaded of himself, so crammed, as he thinks, with excellencies, that it is his grounds of faith that all that look on him love him; and on that vice in him will my revenge find notable cause to work.

**Note: 'Puritan' – a religious person who believed the Church Of England under Elizabeth I retained too many Catholic practices. Puritans were extremely pious and believed in self-restraint. They were against the staging of plays thinking it encouraged immorality. As there is a strong possibility Shakespeare had Catholic sympathies he had a double reason to dislike them.*

SIR TOBY BELCH
What will you do?

SIR TOBY BELCH
What wilt thou do?

MARIA
I'll leave anonymous love letters where he'll find them which complement the colour of his beard, the shapeliness of his leg, the way he walks, the expression in his eyes, his forehead and his appearance, so he'll feel highly flattered. I can write just like my lady, your niece. We can hardly tell our handwriting apart, sometimes we can't remember who wrote what.

MARIA
I will drop in his way some obscure epistles of love, wherein, by the colour of his beard, the shape of his leg, the manner of his gait, the expressure of his eye, forehead, and complexion, he shall find himself most feelingly personated. I can write very like my lady your niece: on a forgotten matter we can hardly make distinction of our hands.

SIR TOBY BELCH
Excellent! I smell a plan coming together.

SIR TOBY BELCH
Excellent! I smell a device.

SIR ANDREW AGUECHEEK
I sense it in my nose too.

SIR TOBY BELCH
He'll think that the letters you'll leave have come from my niece, and that she's in love with him.

MARIA
My idea is indeed along those lines, a horse of the same colour.

SIR ANDREW AGUECHEEK
I have't in my nose too.

SIR TOBY BELCH
He shall think by the letters that thou wilt drop that they come from my niece, and that she's in love with him.

MARIA
My purpose is indeed a horse of that colour.*

**Note: 'Horse of that colour' – a horse of the same colour, a similar idea.*

SIR ANDREW AGUECHEEK
And your horse would make him an ass.

MARIA
Ass, I don't doubt.

SIR ANDREW AGUECHEEK
And your horse now would make him an ass.

MARIA
Ass*, I doubt not.

**Note: 'Ass' – a play on the words 'as' and 'ass' (a stupid or stubborn donkey)*

SIR ANDREW AGUECHEEK
Oh, it will be admirable.

MARIA
A royal sport, I guarantee you. I know my trick will work on him. I'll plant you two where a letter may be found, the fool will make a third, and you can see his reaction to it. But tonight it's to bed, to dream on the scheme. Farewell!

SIR ANDREW AGUECHEEK
O, 'twill be admirable.

MARIA
Sport royal, I warrant you. I know my physic will work with him. I will plant you two, and let the fool make a third*, where he shall find the letter. Observe his construction of it. For this night, to bed*, and dream on* the event. Farewell.

**Note: 'To bed' – in some productions, Sir Toby takes this as an invitation to join Maria in bed, and she pushes him away with the words 'dream on'.*

'Third' – see the note on page 61 about 'we three'.

EXIT MARIA.

SIR TOBY BELCH
(*blows kiss*) Goodnight, queen of the Amazons.

SIR TOBY BELCH
Good night, Penthesilea*.

**Note: 'Penthesilea' – queen of the Amazons, a comical reference to the small stature of Maria. In Greek mythology she helped Troy and was killed by Achilles in the Trojan War.*

SIR ANDREW AGUECHEEK
Upon my soul, she's a good wench!

SIR ANDREW AGUECHEEK
Before me, she's a good wench.

SIR TOBY BELCH She's a pedigree hunting dog tracking her prey, and she adores me, of course.	SIR TOBY BELCH She's a beagle true-bred, and one that adores me. What o' that?*

**Note: 'What o' that?' – a saying meaning naturally, to be expected.*

SIR ANDREW AGUECHEEK I was adored once too.	SIR ANDREW AGUECHEEK I was adored once too.
SIR TOBY BELCH And so to bed, sir knight. You'll need to send for more money.	SIR TOBY BELCH Let's to bed, knight. Thou hadst need send for more money.
SIR ANDREW AGUECHEEK If I can't win over your niece, I'm in a right mess.	SIR ANDREW AGUECHEEK If I cannot recover* your niece, I am a foul way out.

**Note: 'Recover' – gain.*

SIR TOBY BELCH Send for more money, sir knight. If you don't win her in the end, call me an ass.	SIR TOBY BELCH Send for money, knight; if thou hast her not i'th' end, call me cut.*

**Note: 'Cut' – a horse with a docked (removed) tail – a lowly working horse. Used as a term for belittling someone.*

SIR ANDREW AGUECHEEK Trust me, I will if I don't, take it from me.	SIR ANDREW AGUECHEEK If I do not, never trust me, take it how you will.
SIR TOBY BELCH Come, come, I'll mull some wine, it's too late to go to bed now. Come on, sir knight.	SIR TOBY BELCH Come, come, I'll go burn some sack; 'tis too late to go to bed now. Come, knight;

**Note: 'Sack' – dry wine.*

SIR TOBY MAKES TO LEAVE. SIR ANDREW DOESN'T IMMEDIATELY FOLLOW.

SIR TOBY TURNS AND CALLS TO HIM MORE EARNESTLY.

SIR TOBY BELCH (CONT'D) Come on, sir knight.	SIR TOBY BELCH Come, knight.

THEY EXIT, STAGGERING DRUNKENLY

ACT II SCENE IV

A ROOM IN THE DUKE'S PALACE

ENTER DUKE ORSINI, VIOLA (AS CESARIO), CURIO, AND OTHERS.

A BAND OF MUSICIANS ARE PRESENT. ORSINI ADDRESSES THEM.

DUKE ORSINI
(*to Musicians*) Play me some music.
(*to those gathered*) Now, good morning, friends.
(*to Viola*) Now, good Cesario…
(*to Musicians*) Just a piece of that song, the old jolly song we heard last night.
(*to Viola)* I thought it very much lifted my mood, more so than the light airs and frivolous ditties of these brisk and fast-paced times.
(*to Musicians*) Come, just one verse.

DUKE ORSINI
Give me some music. Now good morrow, friends.
Now, good Cesario, but that piece of song,
That old and antic song we heard last night.
Methought it did relieve my passion much,
More than light airs and recollected terms
Of these most brisk and giddy-paced times.
Come, but one verse.

Note: Who Orsini is addressing at any time is a bit vague. His words can be interpreted a number of ways, we can't be sure if any one way is correct. In any production it will be at the directors discretion who Orsino it talking to.

CURIO
The one who sings it is not here, if it pleases your lordship,

CURIO
He is not here, so please your lordship, that should sing it.

DUKE ORSINI
Who is that?

DUKE ORSINI
Who was it?

CURIO
Feste the jester, my lord, a fool that the father of Lady Olivia took much delight in. He is somewhere in the house.

CURIO
Feste* the jester, my lord; a fool that the Lady Olivia's father took much delight in. He is about the house.

**Note: 'Feste the jester' – the only time in the play that Feste is mentioned by name..*

DUKE ORSINI
Find him.
(*to musicians*) And play the tune meanwhile.

DUKE ORSINI
Seek him out, and play the tune the while.

EXIT CURIO.

SOME MUSIC PLAYS.

DUKE ORSINI (CONT'D)
(*to Viola*) Come here, boy. If you should ever fall in love, remember me during the sweet pangs of it. I am like all true lovers, my emotions are all up and down, with the exception of my constant desire for the creature I so love. - How do you like this tune?

VIOLA (AS CESARIO)
It goes straight to the heart of where love is seated.

DUKE ORSINI
You speak like an expert. Upon my life, young though you are, I think your eye has already fallen favourably upon one it adores. Has it not, boy?

VIOLA (AS CESARIO)
A little, with your favourable permission.

DUKE ORSINI
Come hither, boy. If ever thou shalt love,
In the sweet pangs of it remember me;
For such as I am all true lovers are,
Unstaid and skittish in all motions else
Save in the constant image of the creature
That is beloved. How dost thou like this tune?

VIOLA
It gives a very echo to the seat
Where love is throned.

DUKE ORSINI
Thou dost speak masterly.
My life upon't, young though thou art, thine eye
Hath stayed upon some favour that it loves.
Hath it not, boy?

VIOLA
A little, by your favour.*

**Note: 'Favour' – here Viola hints that it is the Duke who is her favourite.*

DUKE ORSINI
What kind of woman is she?

VIOLA (AS CESARIO)
One like you.

DUKE ORSINI
What kind of woman is't?

VIOLA
Of your complexion*.

**Note: 'Complexion' – then meant overall appearance of a person.*

DUKE ORSINI
She is not worthy of you then. How old is she?

VIOLA (AS CESARIO)
About your age, my lord.

DUKE ORSINI
Too old, by heavens. A woman should always marry one older than herself, so she can be more adaptable to him, and keep a steady place in her husband's heart. Because, boy, however much we men praise ourselves, our affections are more fickle and erratic, more intense and wavering, more easily lost and won than women's are.

DUKE ORSINI
She is not worth thee then. What years, i'faith?

VIOLA
About your years, my lord.

DUKE ORSINI
Too old, by heaven. Let still the woman take
An elder than herself: so wears she to him,
So sways she level in her husband's heart.
For, boy, however we do praise ourselves,
Our fancies are more giddy and unfirm,
More longing, wavering, sooner lost and worn*,
Than women's are.

**Note: 'Worn' – modern editions often replace 'worn' with 'won' – being lost and won makes sense of the statement.*

VIOLA (AS CESARIO) I think so too, my lord.	VIOLA I think it well, my lord.
DUKE ORSINI Then let your love be younger than yourself, or your affection will not hold up. You see; *Women, are like roses, whose pretty flower,* *Once it has blossomed, wilts by the hour.*	DUKE ORSINI Then let thy love be younger than thyself*, Or thy affection cannot hold the bent;* *For women are as roses, whose fair flower* *Being once displayed doth fall that very hour.*

**Note: 'Younger than thyself' – Shakespeare's wife, Anne Hathaway, was older by several years. Shakespeare married at 18, his already pregnant bride was 26. If a woman was unmarried at 26 it was difficult to find a husband, especially when she was a lowly milkmaid, so it's possible Shakespeare was seduced into marriage with the encouragement of Anne Hathaway's parents to further their interests and hers, it was an unlikely match. Perhaps some personal sentiment in the phrasing.*

'Hold the bent' – From archery, a bow retaining its springiness when bent to fire.

Note the rhyming couplets from the two as they are talking of love.

VIOLA (AS CESARIO) *And that they do, alas, that is so true!* *To die, when they just to perfection grew.*	VIOLA *And so they are. Alas that they are so! -* *To die, even when they to perfection grow.*

RE-ENTER CURIO WITH FESTE.

DUKE ORSINI NOTICES THEM AND CALLS OUT.

DUKE ORSINI (*to Feste)* Oh, fellow, come, sing the song we heard last night. (*to Cesario*) Listen to it, Cesario, it's old and simple. The wool spinners, the outdoor knitters, and the unmarried maidens who weave their lace with bones all sing it while they work. In truth it's a silly song, it's about the innocence of love as it was in the old days.	DUKE ORSINI O, fellow, come, the song we had last night. Mark it, Cesario, it is old and plain; The spinsters* and the knitters in the sun And the free maids that weave their thread* with bones Do use to chant it. It is silly sooth, And dallies with the innocence of love, Like the old age.

**Note: 'Spinsters' – spinners of wool. It now means an older unmarried woman.*

'Weave their thread' – lace making.

FESTE (*to Orsini*) Are you ready, sir?	FESTE Are you ready, sir?
DUKE ORSINI Yes. Please sing.	DUKE ORSINI Ay; prithee sing.

MUSIC – FESTE SINGS THE SONG.

FESTE

(sings) Come away, come away, death,
And in sad linen let me be laid.
Fly away, fly away, breath,
I am slain by a fair cruel maid.
My shroud of white, adorned with yew,
Oh, prepare it.
And in my death there's none so true
Ever shared it.

Not a flower, not a flower sweet,
On my black coffin let there be strown;
Not a friend, not a friend greet
My poor corpse where my bones shall be thrown.
A thousand, thousand sighs to save,
Lay me, oh, where
My sad true love will ne'er find my grave,
To weep there.

FESTE

[Sings.] *Come away, come away, death,*
And in sad cypress let me be laid.*
Fie away, fie away, breath,*
I am slain by a fair cruel maid.
My shroud of white, stuck all with yew,
O, prepare it.
My part of death no one so true
Did share it.

Not a flower, not a flower sweet,
*On my black coffin let there be strown;**
Not a friend, not a friend greet
My poor corpse where my bones shall be thrown.
A thousand thousand sighs to save,
Lay me, O, where
Sad true lover never find my grave,
To weep there.

> **Note: 'Cypress' – wooden coffin made from cypress tree wood or sheer cloth used to wrap a body in. As is mentions shroud shortly after and coffin in the next verse, cloth is more likely.*
>
> *'Fie away' – many modern editions change this to 'fly away', it could equally be 'die away'.*
>
> *'Strown' – old version of strewn, which means scattered.*

DUKE ORSINI
Take this for your trouble.

DUKE ORSINI
There's for thy pains.

THE DUKE OFFERS FESTE MONEY.

FESTE DECLINES TAKING IT.

FESTE
No trouble, sir. I take pleasure in singing, sir.

FESTE
No pains, sir; I take pleasure in singing, sir.

THE DUKE OFFERS FESTE MONEY AGAIN.

DUKE ORSINI
I'll pay for your pleasure then.

DUKE ORSINI
I'll pay thy pleasure then.

FESTE
Truly, sir, pleasure pays for itself one way or another.

FESTE
Truly, sir, and pleasure will be paid one time or another.

DUKE ORSINI
(*dismissing him*) Then now I am done with you.

DUKE ORSINI
Give me now leave to leave thee.

FESTE

May the god of sadness protect you, and your tailor make your waistcoat of multi-coloured silk, because your mind is as changeable as the colour of opal. I would have men of that inconsistency sent to sea, then their interests could be anything and their destinations everywhere and nowhere. That's what it takes to make a good voyage seeking nothing.
Farewell.

FESTE

Now the melancholy god protect thee, and the tailor make thy doublet of changeable taffeta*, for thy mind is a very opal*. I would have men of such constancy put to sea, that their business might be everything and their intent everywhere*, for that's it that always makes a good voyage of nothing*. Farewell.

**Note: 'Changeable taffeta' – shot silk, it changes colour depending on the angle it is viewed, as opal does. The Duke's mind is similarly changeable, he wanted Feste to sing and now wants him to leave.*

'Intent everywhere' – from an old proverb – 'He that is everywhere is nowhere'.

'Nothing' – double meaning of pursuing female genitalia. A man has something between his legs, a woman has nothing – her nothing, often used by Shakespeare to bypass obscenity laws.

DUKE ORSINI

Let everyone else retire as well.

DUKE ORSINI

Let all the rest give place.

EXIT ALL BUT DUKE ORSINI AND VIOLA (AS CESARIO).

DUKE ORSINI (CONT'D)

Once again, Cesario, go to that supreme lady so unrivalled in her cruelty. Tell her my love is the noblest in the world, and places no more heed to the land and riches fortune has bestowed upon her than it does to unpredictable fortune itself. Rather, it is the miracle of beauty, the most valuable gem of all, that nature has adorned her with which attracts my soul.

DUKE ORSINI

Once more, Cesario,
Get thee to yond same sovereign cruelty.
Tell her my love, more noble than the world,
Prizes not quantity of dirty lands.
The parts that fortune hath bestowed upon her,
Tell her I hold as giddily as fortune;
But 'tis that miracle and queen of gems
That nature pranks her in attracts my soul.

VIOLA (AS CESARIO)

What if she cannot love you, sir?

VIOLA

But if she cannot love you, sir?

DUKE ORSINI

I cannot accept this answer.

DUKE ORSINI

I cannot be so answered.

VIOLA (AS CESARIO)

Truly, you must. What if some lady, as perhaps there may be, (*meaning herself*) longs for your love with great pangs of her heart, just as you have for Olivia. You cannot love her, and you tell her so. She has to accept your answer.

VIOLA

Sooth, but you must.
Say that some lady, as perhaps there is,*
Hath for your love as great a pang of heart
As you have for Olivia - you cannot love her;
You tell her so - must she not then be answered?

**Note: 'Some lady… hath for your love' – she means herself.*

DUKE ORSINI
There is no woman whose body can bear the beating of such a strong passion within as the love which burdens my heart. No woman's heart is big enough to contain such passion. They are incapable of holding so much love inside. Sad to say, their love is like an appetite which does not please the stomach, just the hunger, which suffering from excess causes nausea and revulsion. But my appetite is as hungry as the ocean, and can digest it all. Make no comparisons between the love a woman can have for me with the love I have for Olivia.

DUKE ORSINI
There is no woman's sides
Can bide the beating of so strong a passion
As love doth give my heart; no woman's heart
So big to hold so much: they lack retention.
Alas, their love may be called appetite,
No motion of the liver, but the palate,
That suffer surfeit, cloyment, and revolt;
But mine is all as hungry as the sea,
And can digest as much. Make no compare
Between that love a woman can bear me
And that I owe Olivia.

VIOLA (AS CESARIO)
Yes, but I know…

VIOLA
Ay, but I know -

VIOLA STOPS.
SHE WAS ABOUT TO SAY SHE KNOWS OF JUST SUCH A WOMAN (HER) BUT REALISES SHE CANNOT REVEAL WHO WITHOUT GIVING THE GAME AWAY.

DUKE ORSINI
What do you know?

DUKE ORSINI
What dost thou know?

VIOLA (AS CESARIO)
I know too well the love a woman may hold for a man, Indeed, they can have as true a heart as we do. My father had a daughter who loved a man, just as perhaps, if I were a woman, I would hold for your lordship.

VIOLA
Too well what love women to men may owe.
In faith, they are as true of heart as we.
My father had a daughter loved a man,
As it might be perhaps, were I a woman,
I should your lordship.

DUKE ORSINI
And what happened with her love?

DUKE ORSINI
And what's her history?

VIOLA (AS CESARIO)
Nothing, my lord. She never revealed her love, she kept it concealed, like a hidden grub in a rose bud it fed on the bloom of her cheek. She pined in her thoughts, and in sickness and sadness she sat like the statue of Patience, suffering her grief. Was this not true love? We men may say more, swear our love more, but indeed our outward pourings are greater than our love, as we often boast more in our promises than exists in our love.

VIOLA
A blank, my lord. She never told her love,
But let concealment, like a worm i'th bud,
Feed on her damask cheek. She pined in thought,
And with a green and yellow melancholy
She sat like Patience on a monument,
Smiling at grief. Was not this love indeed?
We men may say more, swear more, but indeed
Our shows are more than will, for still we prove
Much in our vows, but little in our love.

DUKE ORSINI
Did your sister die of her love, my boy?

DUKE ORSINI
But died thy sister of her love, my boy?

VIOLA (AS CESARIO)
I am all the daughters my father has and all the brothers too, though I can't be sure.
Sir, shall I go to this lady?

VIOLA
I am all the daughters of my father's house,
And all the brothers too; and yet I know not.*
Sir, shall I to this lady?

**Note: An ambiguous statement, while not being untrue. She still holds out hope for her brother's survival. It also suggests to Orsini that the sister in her story may have died of a broken heart.*

DUKE ORSINI
Yes, that's the plan.
Go there in haste, and give her this jewel.
My love's here to stay, so return no denial.

DUKE ORSINI
Ay, that's the theme.
To her in haste. Give her this jewel. Say*
My love can give no place, bide no denay.

DUKE ORSINI HANDS A JEWEL TO VIOLA (AS CESARIO).

**Note: 'Jewel' – The Duke hands Viola the jewel to give to Olivia, but the jewel is not mentioned again. The next time they meet, Viola only gives back the ring Olivia sent her.*

The scene ends on a rhyming couplet.

ACT II SCENE V

OLIVIA'S GARDEN.

ENTER SIR TOBY, SIR ANDREW, AND FABIAN (A SERVANT TO OLIVIA).

SIR TOBY BELCH Come along, Signore Fabian.	SIR TOBY BELCH Come thy ways, Signor Fabian.
FABIAN I'm coming all right. If I miss the tiniest part of this fun let me be boiled to death with melancholy.	FABIAN Nay, I'll come. If I lose a scruple of this sport let me be boiled* to death with melancholy.*

**Note: 'Boiled' – boil was pronounced bile back then. A pun, as bile was thought of as the source of melancholy. Melancholy is deep sadness or depression.*

SIR TOBY BELCH Would you not be glad to see that mean dog of a whore-monger fall upon some public shame?	SIR TOBY BELCH Wouldst thou not be glad to have the niggardly rascally sheep-biter come by some notable shame?

**Note: 'Sheep-biter' had the meaning of either a dog which attacked (worried) sheep, or as a term of abuse for a puritan – especially hypocritical puritans who preached the absence of sex outside of marriage while they themselves slept with prostitutes. Mutton (the meat of adult sheep) was a term for a whore.*

FABIAN I would rejoice, man! You know he drove me out of favour with my lady because of some bear-baiting we held here.	FABIAN I would exult, man. You know he brought me out o' favour with my lady about a bear-baiting* here.

**Note: 'Bear-baiting' – see note in Act I scene III, page 30.*

SIR TOBY BELCH To annoy him we'll bring the bear back again, and we'll make a complete fool of him. Shall we not, Sir Andrew?	SIR TOBY BELCH To anger him we'll have the bear again, and we will fool him black-and-blue. Shall we not, Sir Andrew?
SIR ANDREW AGUECHEEK If we do not it will be the regret of our lives.	SIR ANDREW AGUECHEEK And we do not, it is pity of our lives.

ENTER MARIA CARRYING A LETTER.

SIR TOBY BELCH Here comes the little villain. (*to Maria*) How is my exotic gem?	SIR TOBY BELCH Here comes the little villain. How now, my metal of India?

Malvolio is on his way

MARIA
All three of you hide behind the box-tree. Malvolio's coming down this path. He's been in the sunshine practising grovelling courtesies to his own shadow this last half hour. If you have a love of mockery observe him, as I know this letter will make a complete idiot of him. Keep out of sight, do not give the game away!

MARIA
Get ye all three into the box-tree. Malvolio's coming down this walk. He has been yonder i'the sun practising behaviour to his own shadow this half hour. Observe him, for the love of mockery, for I know this letter will make a contemplative idiot of him. Close, in the name of jesting!

MARIA DROPS THE LETTER ON THE PATH.

MARIA (CONT'D)
Lie low, here comes the trout that must be caught by tickling.

MARIA
Lie thou there; for here comes the trout that must be caught with tickling.*

**Note: 'Tickling' – An old way of catching trout in a river (still used today) was to place your hand in the water and caress the fish with the fingers as if tickling it and then swipe it out of the water.*

EXIT MARIA AS THE MEN CONCEAL THEMSELVES.

ENTER MALVOLIO WALKING DOWN THE PATH LOST IN HIS THOUGHTS.
HE IS IMAGINING LIFE MARRIED TO OLIVIA.

MALVOLIO
(*speaking his thoughts to what he thinks is only himself*) It's just fortune, all just fortune. Maria once told me that Olivia was fond of me, and I myself have heard her say that should she fall in love it would be with someone very like myself. And she treats me with greater respect that any of her other staff. What should I make of that?

MALVOLIO
'Tis but fortune, all is fortune*. Maria once told me she did affect me; and I have heard herself come thus near, that, should she fancy, it should be one of my complexion. Besides, she uses me with a more exalted respect than anyone else that follows her. What should I think on't?

**Note: 'Fortune' – the triple meaning of which is fate, good luck and a large sum of money.*

SIR TOBY BELCH
What a conceited rogue.

FABIAN
Keep quiet! His contemplations make a vain turkey-cock of him. Look how he struts under his stuck-up plumes!

SIR TOBY BELCH
Here's an overweening rogue.

FABIAN
O, peace! Contemplation makes a rare turkey-cock* of him. How he jets under his advanced plumes!

**Note: 'Turkey-cock' a proverbial vain bird which struts around showing off its plumage.*

SIR ANDREW AGUECHEEK
By god, I could so beat the rogue.

SIR ANDREW AGUECHEEK
'Slight, I could so beat the rogue.

SIR TOBY BELCH
Quiet, I say.

MALVOLIO
(*imagining*) To be Count Malvolio.

SIR TOBY BELCH
Huh! Rogue!

SIR ANDREW AGUECHEEK
Shoot him, shoot him.

SIR TOBY BELCH
Peace, I say.

MALVOLIO
To be Count Malvolio.

SIR TOBY BELCH
Ah, rogue!

SIR ANDREW AGUECHEEK
Pistol him*, pistol him.

**Note:* *'Pistol him' – shoot him as if he is the game bird he acts like.*

SIR TOBY BELCH
Quiet, Quiet.

MALVOLIO
(*aside*) There are examples of it happening. Lady Strachy married the man in charge of her wardrobe.

SIR ANDREW AGUECHEEK
A pox on him, the Jezebel!

SIR TOBY BELCH
Peace, peace.

MALVOLIO
There is example for't: the Lady of the Strachy married the yeoman of the wardrobe.

SIR ANDREW AGUECHEEK
Fie on him, Jezebel!*

**Note:* *'Jezebel' – a shameful woman, named after the biblical wicked wife of King Ahab. If he is calling Lady Strachy a Jezebel then Olivia is no different.*

FABIAN
Keep quiet! Now he's deep in thought, look how his imagination inflates his pride.

MALVOLIO
(*aside*) When I've been married to her for three months, sitting on my throne…

SIR TOBY BELCH
Oh, for a catapult to stone him in the eye!

FABIAN
O peace! Now he's deeply in; look how imagination blows him.

MALVOLIO
Having been three months married to her, sitting in my state -

SIR TOBY BELCH
O for a stone-bow* to hit him in the eye!

**Note:* *'Stone-bow' – a crossbow modified to fire stones..*

MALVOLIO
…ordering my officials around me, in my ornately embroidered velvet gown, having come from a chaise longue where I have left Olivia sleeping…

MALVOLIO
Calling my officers about me, in my branched velvet gown, having come from a day-bed* where I have left Olivia sleeping -

**Note:* *'Day-bed' – chaise longue (a long sofa with an armrest at one end only). He imagines he has left a satisfied Olivia sleeping after having made love to her in the daytime.*

SIR TOBY BELCH
Fire and brimstone!

SIR TOBY BELCH
Fire and brimstone!*

**Note: 'Fire and brimstone' the supposed torments awaiting those who go to hell.*

FABIAN
Oh, quiet, quiet!

FABIAN
O peace, peace!

MALVOLIO
...and then I adopt a stately manner, and after sternly looking them over one by one, tell them I know my place, as they should do theirs, and order them to summon my relation, Toby...

MALVOLIO
And then to have the humour of state; and after a demure travel of regard, telling them I know my place, as I would they should do theirs, to ask for my kinsman Toby* -

**Note: 'Toby' – he deliberately drops the title of 'Sir', and comments how Sir Toby will be related to him (by marriage to Lady Olivia).*

SIR TOBY BELCH
Chain him up!

SIR TOBY BELCH
Bolts and shackles!*

**Note: 'Bolts and shackles' – used to restrain prisoners.*

FABIAN
Quiet, quiet, quiet! Now, now !

FABIAN
O peace, peace, peace! Now, now!

MALVOLIO WALKS CLOSE TO THE LETTER BUT DOESN'T NOTICE IT YET.

MALVOLIO
...Seven of my staff jump obediently to attention and go fetch him. I keep an austere look, and maybe wind up my pocket watch, or play with some rich jewel...

MALVOLIO
Seven of my people, with an obedient start, make out for him. I frown the while, and perchance wind up my watch, or play with my -some rich jewel. Toby approaches, curtsies there to me -

HE TOUCHES HIS STEWARD'S CHAIN ABSENTMINDEDLY, THEN REALISES IT IS A REMINDER OF HIS CURRENT POSITION AND HURRIEDLY DROPS IT.

MALVOLIO (CONT'D)
...Toby approaches and bows to me...

MALVOLIO
Toby approaches, curtsies there to me -

SIR TOBY BELCH
Should this fellow be allowed to live?

SIR TOBY BELCH
Shall this fellow live?

FABIAN
Even if wild horses try to drag the words out of us, keep quiet!

FABIAN
Though our silence be drawn from us with cars, yet peace.

MALVOLIO
...I extend my hand to him like so...

MALVOLIO
I extend my hand to him thus...

MALVOLIO EXTENDS A LIMP HAND.

MALVOLIO (CONT'D) …suppressing my usual smile with a severe look of authority…	MALVOLIO ...quenching my familiar smile with a austere regard of control -
SIR TOBY BELCH (*hushed*) And then 'Toby' strikes you a blow to the chops.	SIR TOBY BELCH And does not Toby take you a blow o'the lips then?
MALVOLIO …saying "Cousin Toby, since good fortune has cast me upon your niece, I have the authority to say this"…	MALVOLIO Saying "Cousin Toby, my fortunes having cast me on your niece, give me this prerogative of speech" -
SIR TOBY BELCH Say what?	SIR TOBY BELCH What, what?
MALVOLIO (*pompously*) …"You must curb your drunkenness."…	MALVOLIO "You must amend your drunkenness."
SIR TOBY BELCH Get away with you, you rogue!	SIR TOBY BELCH Out, scab!

ANGERED, SIR TOBY ATTEMPTS TO RISE TO CONFRONT MALVOLIO.

FABIAN RESTRAINS HIM.

FABIAN No, be patient, or we'll ruin our plot.	FABIAN Nay, patience, or we break the sinews of our plot.
MALVOLIO … "Besides, you waste your valuable time with that foolish knight"…	MALVOLIO "Besides, you waste the treasure of your time with a foolish knight" -
SIR ANDREW AGUECHEEK That's me, I'll bet.	SIR ANDREW AGUECHEEK That's me, I warrant you.
MALVOLIO … "The one called Sir Andrew"…	MALVOLIO "One Sir Andrew" -
SIR ANDREW AGUECHEEK It knew it was me, because people often call me foolish.	SIR ANDREW AGUECHEEK I knew 'twas I, for many do call me fool.

MALVOLIO SEES THE LETTER ON THE GROUND.

MALVOLIO Now what have we here?	MALVOLIO What employment have we here?

MALVOLIO PICKS UP THE LETTER FROM THE GROUND.

FABIAN Now the dumb bird is entering the snare.	FABIAN Now is the woodcock* near the gin*.

**Note: 'Woodcock' – famously stupid bird.*

'Gin' – gin trap. A metal sprung trap that was left to catch birds or animals

SIR TOBY BELCH Quiet! May the god of mischief compel him to read it out loud!	SIR TOBY BELCH O, peace! And the spirit of humours intimate reading aloud to him!

MALVOLIO STUDIES THE OUTER WRITING.

MALVOLIO Upon my life, this is my ladyship's handwriting. These are her C's, her U's, and her T's, and here she makes her big P's. It is beyond doubt her writing.	MALVOLIO [*Taking up the letter.*] By my life, this is my lady's hand. These be her very C's, her U's, and her T's, and thus makes she her great P's. It is in contempt of question her hand.
SIR ANDREW AGUECHEEK Her C's, her U's, and her T's? Why those?	SIR ANDREW AGUECHEEK Her C's, her U's, and her T's?* Why that?

**Note: 'C U T' – a bawdy reference. 'Cut' was slang for a ladies genitals - where she Pees from (P's). The audience would find Sir Andrew's ignorance amusing, and him repeating the letters made doubly sure the audience did not miss the joke.*

MALVOLIO *(reads aloud)* "*To my secret beloved, this letter, and my fond wishes.*" It's the way she talks! Excuse me, wax…	MALVOLIO [Reads.] "To the unknown beloved, this, and my good wishes." Her very phrases! By your leave, wax.

HE BREAKS OPEN THE WAX SEAL OF THE ENVELOPE.

MALVOLIO (CONT'D) Carefully does it! And the stamp in the wax is of Lucrece. That's her seal – it's from my lady. Who is it too though?	MALVOLIO Soft! And the impressure her Lucrece,* with which she uses to seal* - 'tis my lady. To whom should this be?

**Note: 'Lucrece' – A woman of virtue and chastity who killed herself after being raped by the Roman soldier, Tarquin. Shakespeare had written a poem titled 'The Rape Of Lucrece', one of his earliest works, and it is also mentioned in five of his plays.*

'Impressure… seal' – a personal stamped imprint in melted wax to seal an envelope closed.

FABIAN This will win him over, heart and soul.	FABIAN This wins him, liver and all.

MALVOLIO STARTS READING THE LETTER OUT LOUD.

MALVOLIO *(reads) "God knows I'm in love. But with who? Lips, do not move. No man must know."*	MALVOLIO *[Reads.] "Jove knows I love;* But who? Lips, do not move;* No man must know."*

**Note: Back then 'love' rhymed with 'move'.*

MALVOLIO (CONT'D) *(thoughtfully) "No man must know."* What follows that? The rhythm changes! (*he ponders*) *"No man must know."* Could this be about you, Malvolio!	MALVOLIO *"No man must know."* What follows? The numbers altered! *"No man must know."** If this should be thee, Malvolio!

**Note: 'No man must know' – he possibly realises that this sounds like 'Malvolio'.*

SIR TOBY BELCH May you be hanged, you stinking badger.	SIR TOBY BELCH Marry, hang thee, brock!*

**Note: "Brock' – badger – often referred to as 'stinking brock'.*

MALVOLIO *(reads) "I command the one I adore, But silence, like Lucrece's knife, With bloodless stroke my heart does gore. M.O.A.I. does lead my life."*	MALVOLIO *[Reads.]"I may command where I adore, But silence, like a Lucrece knife, With bloodless stroke my heart doth gore.* M.O.A.I. *doth sway my life."*
FABIAN An absurd yet clever riddle.	FABIAN A fustian riddle.
SIR TOBY BELCH An excellent wench, is Maria.	SIR TOBY BELCH Excellent wench, say I.
MALVOLIO *"M.O.A.I. does lead my life."* But let me think, let me think, let me think.	MALVOLIO "M.O.A.I. doth sway my life." Nay, but first let me see, let me see, let me see.
FABIAN What poisonous dish has she prepared for him?	FABIAN What dish o' poison has she dressed him!
SIR TOBY BELCH And at that point the kestrel's flight is diverted!	SIR TOBY BELCH And with what wing the staniel* checks* at it!

**Note: "Staniel' – Kestrel. While pursuing its prey it 'checks' (gets distracted) and turns to pursue something else. Another of Shakespeare's regular hawking references.*

MALVOLIO
"I may command the one 'I' adore."
(*sudden thought*) She commands me! I serve her. She is my lady. This is evident to anyone with a brain, this is not difficult to fathom out. What about the end? What do those letters represent? If I could somehow relate them to me… wait…
(*trying to figure it out*) "*M.O.A.I.*"

MALVOLIO
"I may command where I adore."
Why, she may command me: I serve her, she is my lady. Why, this is evident to any formal capacity; there is no obstruction in this. And the end; what should that alphabetical position portend? If I could make that resemble something in me. Softly -
"M.O.A.I."

SIR TOBY BELCH
(*mimicking two of the letters*) Oh, ay, make sense of that. Now the scent has gone cold.

SIR TOBY BELCH
O, ay, make up that. He is now at a cold scent.*

**Note: 'Cold scent' - hunting dogs pursuing their prey lose the scent.*

FABIAN
Despite this the hound dog will pick up the scent again, after all it's so obvious it stinks like a fox.

FABIAN
Sowter* will cry* upon't for all this, though it be as rank as a fox.

**Note: 'Sowter' – a hunting hound.*

'Cry' – A pack of hunting hounds and the sounds they make while tracking the scent of a fox.

MALVOLIO
"*M*" – Malvolio! M, that's the first letter of my name.

MALVOLIO
"M" - Malvolio! M, why, that begins my name.

FABIAN
Didn't I say he would work it out? The dog is good at breaks in the scent.

FABIAN
Did not I say he would work it out? The cur is excellent at faults.*

**Note: 'Faults' – gaps in the scent the hounds are following.*

MALVOLIO
"*M*" – But that doesn't make sense of what follows it. That falls apart under examination. '*A*' should follow, but '*O*' does.

MALVOLIO
"M" - But then there is no consonancy in the sequel; that suffers under probation. 'A' should follow, but 'O' does.

FABIAN
And it will end in the O of a noose', I hope.

FABIAN
And O shall end, I hope.

SIR TOBY BELCH
Yes, or I'll beat him and make him cry "Oh!"

SIR TOBY BELCH
Ay, or I'll cudgel him, and make him cry "O!"

MALVOLIO
But "*I*" comes at the end.

MALVOLIO
And then 'I' comes behind.

FABIAN
Aye, and if you had an 'eye' in the back of your head you'd see more mockery at your heels than fortunes ahead of you.

FABIAN
Ay, and you had any eye behind you you might see more detraction at your heels* than fortunes before you.

them hiding

**Note: 'At your heels' – the men who are hiding behind him, causing mischief.*

MALVOLIO
"*M.O.A.I.*" This code is not so easy to break as the previous, and yet if I bend the rules a little, it could refer to me, as every one of these letters is in my name. Wait… some writing follows.

(*reads aloud*) *"If this should fall into your hands, ponder this. In my position in life I am above you, but do not be afraid of greatness. Some are born great, some achieve greatness, and some have greatness thrust upon them. Fate awaits you with open arms, let your soul and spirit embrace it, and to accustom yourself to what you are likely to become, cast off your humble demeaner and be born anew."*

MALVOLIO
"M.O.A.I." This simulation is not as the former; and yet, to crush this a little, it would bow to me, for every one of these letters are in my name. Soft, here follows prose.

[Reads.] *"If this fall into thy hand, revolve. In my stars I am above thee, but be not afraid of greatness. Some are born great, some achieve greatness, and some have greatness thrust upon 'em. Thy Fates* open their hands; let thy blood and spirit embrace them; and, to inure thyself to what thou art like to be, cast thy humble slough* and appear fresh.*

MALVOLIO PAUSES A MOMENT TAKING IN WHAT HE HAS READ.

**Note: 'Fates' - in mythology, life span is determined by the three Fates. One spins a thread, one assigns it to a person, the other cuts it. The length determining the person's lifespan.*

'Slough' – the old skin cast off by a snake in order to renew it.

'M.O.A.I.' – a code which has had scholars disagreeing for centuries. The most likely conclusion is that it stands for the Latin phrase 'Manus Osculatione Aspectu Itali', which translates to 'Hand, Kiss, Look of an Italian'.

This expression would have been aimed at Queen Elizabeth I who the play was first performed before. Briefly: a flamboyant courtier, Harvey, eager to further himself in the royal court, and dressed outrageously, read a Latin poem he had written to the Queen. The Queen remarked after the recitation that Harvey 'Looks like an Italian", and followed this by ordering him to kiss her hand.

This episode was mocked in society papers. In the publication 'Have with you to Saffron-Walden', the author, Nashe, misquoted Harvey, altering the order of the hand kiss and the Italian look. However, Shakespeare would not have known this, and M.O.A.I. would have been recognised by the Queen, who was fond of wordplay and fluent in many languages.

Further evidence is seen in Malvolio having an Italian name, the ridiculous outfit he would wear before the countess (just as Harvey had done before Elizabeth I), and Maria calling him 'Signor', referring to his 'Italian love', and ending her letter with the phrase 'not worthy to touch fortune's fingers.

Or it could simply be the first, last, second first, and second last letters of 'Malvolio'. A cryptic plus a simple solution to cater for all levels of audience.

MALVOLIO (CONT'D)
(*reads aloud*) "*She that yearns for you gives you this advice - antagonise a kinsman and be surly with servants. Let your tongue ring out with political arguments, adopt the role of one above others. Remember who praised your yellow tights and wished to see you always cross-gartered. Make sure you remember. So, you can have it all if you want, if not, stay a steward forever with your fellow servants, not worthy to touch the hand of fortune. Farewell. She who would swap positions to be with you.*
The Unhappy Fortunate One."

MALVOLIO
[Reads.] "Be opposite with a kinsman, surly with servants. Let thy tongue tang arguments of state; put thyself into the trick of singularity. She thus advises thee that sighs for thee. Remember who commended thy yellow stockings and wished to see thee ever cross-gartered*. I say, remember. Go to, thou art made if thou desir'st to be so; if not, let me see thee a steward still, the fellow of servants, and not worthy to touch Fortune's* fingers. Farewell. She that would alter services* with thee,*
The Fortunate Unhappy."

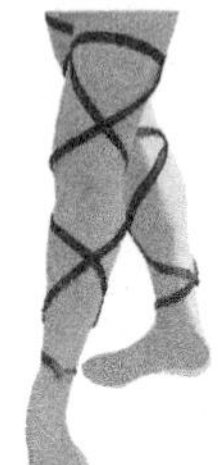
Cross-gartered

**Note: 'Kinsman' – meaning Sir Toby.*

'Cross gartered' – straps which crossed the tights, often with a bow at the knee. Flamboyant fashion for young bachelors.

'Fortune' - The Goddess of luck and chance. She had a wheel she turned, people on one side were on the way up, the other side were on the way down. Up or down on their luck.

'Alter services' – swap roles. When married the husband became the master of the household.

Wheel Of Fortune

MALVOLIO (CONT'D)
(*aside*) This is as plain as daylight in open country! This is obvious. I *will* be aloof, I *will* read weighty political tomes, I *will* antagonise Sir Toby, I *will* wash my hands of lowly acquaintances, I *will* be in every smallest detail a gentleman. I'm not fooling myself now, my imagination is not running away with me, now, every reason stirs me up in the belief that my lady loves me. She *did* praise my yellow tights recently, she *did* praise my legs being cross-gartered, and in doing so she reveals her love for me, and with heavy hints she guides me to adopt the habits which are to her liking. I thank my lucky stars, I *am* fortunate. I *will* be distant, strong, and wear my yellow cross-gartered tights, just as fast as I can put them on. Heavens and my lucky stars be praised!

MALVOLIO
Daylight and champaign discovers not more! This is open. I will be proud, I will read politic authors, I will baffle Sir Toby, I will wash off gross acquaintance, I will be point-device* the very man. I do not now fool myself, to let imagination jade me; for every reason excites to this, that my lady loves me. She did commend my yellow stockings of late, she did praise my leg being cross-gartered, and in this she manifests herself to my love, and with a kind of injunction drives me to these habits of her liking. I thank my stars, I am happy. I will be strange, stout, in yellow stockings, and cross-gartered, even with the swiftness of putting on. Jove and my stars be praised!

**Note: 'Point-device' – refers to the precision of detail in fine embroidery.*

MALVOLIO (CONT'D)
(*turning the page*) There is a postscript as well. (*reads*) "*You cannot help but know who I am. If you return my love, let it show by smiling – your smile is becoming of you. Therefore in my presence always smile, my dearest sweet, I beg of you.*"

MALVOLIO
Here is yet a postscript.
[Reads.] "Thou canst not choose but know who I am. If thou entertain'st my love, let it appear in thy smiling: thy smiles become thee well. Therefore in my presence still smile, dear my sweet, I prithee."

MALVOLIO LOOKS UP TO THE SKIES.

MALVOLIO (CONT'D)
Heavens, I thank you. I *will* smile,
(*he makes a very forced smile*)
I *will* do everything that you wish of me.

MALVOLIO
Jove, I thank thee. I will smile; I will do everything that thou wilt have me.

EXIT MALVOLIO SMILING GROTESQUELY.

FABIAN
I *will* not give up my part of this prank even for a pension of thousands from the Shah of Persia.

SIR TOBY BELCH
I could marry that wench for this prank.

SIR ANDREW AGUECHEEK
So could I too.

SIR TOBY BELCH
And ask for no other dowry from her than to be in on another prank like this.

SIR ANDREW AGUECHEEK
Nor I neither.

FABIAN
I will not give my part of this sport for a pension of thousands to be paid from the Sophy.

SIR TOBY BELCH
I could marry this wench for this device.

SIR ANDREW AGUECHEEK
So could I too.

SIR TOBY BELCH
And ask no other dowry with her but such another jest.

SIR ANDREW AGUECHEEK
Nor I neither.

RE-ENTER MARIA.

FABIAN
Here comes my noble trickster of fools.

SIR TOBY BELCH
(*to Maria*) Shall I prostate myself before you?

SIR ANDREW AGUECHEEK
And shall I too?

FABIAN
Here comes my noble gull-catcher.*

SIR TOBY BELCH
Wilt thou set thy foot o' my neck?*

SIR ANDREW AGUECHEEK
Or o' mine either?

**Note: 'Gull' – a proverbial stupid bird.*

'Foot o' my neck' – Symbolic of being a slave, under her foot.

SIR TOBY BELCH
Shall I stake my freedom on the throw of a dice, and become your slave if I lose?

SIR TOBY BELCH
Shall I play* my freedom at tray-trip*, and become thy bond-slave?

**Note: 'Play' – wager.*

'Tray-trip' – A dice game requiring throwing a three to win.

SIR ANDREW AGUECHEEK
Indeed, shall I too?

SIR ANDREW AGUECHEEK
I'faith, or I either?

SIR TOBY BELCH
You have put in him such a vision that when he learns the truth he will be driven mad.

SIR TOBY BELCH
Why, thou hast put him in such a dream that when the image of it leaves him he must run mad.

MARIA
Yes, but tell me truly, did it work on him?

MARIA
Nay, but say true, does it work upon him?

SIR TOBY BELCH
Like brandy to a midwife.

SIR TOBY BELCH
Like aqua-vitae with a midwife.*

**Note: 'Midwife' – in Elizabethan England a midwife was the best job a woman could hold. It was a high pressure job, deaths of infants and mothers were high and doctors usually had no involvement in childbirth. Germs were not known about so hygiene was poor and in the event of complications midwives were not able to perform Caesarean sections. Midwives had to swear a detailed oath to receive a licence to operate from the archbishop of Canterbury, this had been introduced to stop the practice by inexperienced and often incompetent women.*

Women only started giving birth lying on their backs in the last 300 years.. Before this in England a birthing chair was common.

MARIA
If you want to see the results of the prank, watch his first meeting with my lady. He will come before her in yellow tights, which is a colour she loathes, and cross-gartered, which she also detests, and he will smile at her, which will be so inappropriate for her current mood - being permanently depressed as she is - that it cannot fail to turn him into a figure of scorn. If you want to see it, follow me.

MARIA
If you will then see the fruits of the sport, mark his first approach before my lady. He will come to her in yellow stockings, and 'tis a colour she abhors, and cross-gartered, a fashion she detests; and he will smile upon her, which will now be so unsuitable to her disposition, being addicted to a melancholy as she is, that it cannot but turn him into a notable contempt. If you will see it, follow me.

SIR TOBY BELCH
To the gates of hell, you most excellent devil of witty mischief!

SIR TOBY BELCH
To the gates of Tartar*, thou most excellent devil of wit.

**Note: 'Tartar' – Tartarus, classical hell. A part of the underworld in mythology where the wicked suffered punishment for their misdeeds.*

EXIT SIR TOBY FOLLOWING MARIA.

SIR ANDREW AGUECHEEK	SIR ANDREW AGUECHEEK
I'll be one and go along too.	I'll make one too.*

**Note: 'One too' – a play on the numbers one and two.*

EXIT SIR ANDREW RUNNING BEHIND AND FABIAN BRINGING UP THE REAR.

ACT III

ILLYRIA

OLIVIA'S RESIDENCE

"IF ONE SHOULD BE A PREY, HOW MUCH THE BETTER TO FALL BEFORE THE LION THAN THE WOLF"

ACT III

ACT III SCENE I

OLIVIA'S GARDEN.

ENTER VIOLA (AS CESARIO)
AND FROM A DIFFERENT DIRECTION, ENTER
FESTE PLAYING A TABOR (PIPE) AND DRUM.

VIOLA (AS CESARIO) God bless you, friend, and your music too. Is your living by your music?	VIOLA Save thee, friend, and thy music. Dost thou live by thy tabor?
FESTE No, sir, my living is by the church.	FESTE No, sir, I live by the church.
VIOLA (AS CESARIO) Are you a man of the clergy?	VIOLA Art thou a churchman?*

**Note: As Feste is dressed in his fools clothes this will be seen as a joke by the audience.*

FESTE Not at all, sir. I am living by the church, because I am living at my house, and my house stands by the church.	FESTE No such matter, sir. I do live by the church, for I do live at my house, and my house doth stand by the church.
VIOLA (AS CESARIO) So you are saying that a king sleeps with a beggar if a beggar lives near him, or the church stands by your drum if your drum stands by the church.	VIOLA So thou mayst say the king lies by a beggar if a beggar dwell near him, or the church stands by thy tabor if thy tabor stand by the church.
FESTE You have it, sir. To see such wit at this age! A sentence is like a kid leather glove to a quick mind – quickly turned inside out.	FESTE You have said, sir. To see this age! A sentence is but a chev'ril glove to a good wit - how quickly the wrong side may be turned outward!
VIOLA (AS CESARIO) Yes, that's true. Those who cleverly play with words can quickly make them lewd.	VIOLA Nay, that's certain. They that dally nicely with words may quickly make them wanton.
FESTE In that case I wish my sister had no name, sir.	FESTE I would therefore my sister had had no name, sir.

VIOLA (AS CESARIO) Why not, man?	VIOLA Why, man?
FESTE Well, sir, because her name is a word, which with wordplay would make my sister lewd. But then again words are deceptive rascals ever since legal contracts put them to shame.	FESTE Why, sir, her name's a word, and to dally with that word might make my sister wanton. But indeed words are very rascals since bonds disgraced them.
VIOLA (AS CESARIO) Your reasoning, man?	VIOLA Thy reason, man?
FESTE In truth, sir, I can't give you any without using words, and words have now grown so false that I am loath to prove my reasoning with them.	FESTE Troth, sir, I can yield you none without words, and words are grown so false I am loath to prove reason* with them.

**Note: 'Reason' – throughout the play, Feste plays with words often using obscure reasoning and elaborate syllogisms (where a conclusion is drawn whether valid or not) to come to his conclusion.*

He mentions that words are deceptive and false, so they are of no value unless contained in a legally binding contract.

VIOLA (AS CESARIO) I'll bet you are a fellow of good cheer who cares for nothing.	VIOLA I warrant thou art a merry fellow, and car'st for nothing*.
FESTE Not so, sir, I do care for something, but in my mind, sir, I do not care for you. If that means I care for nothing, sir, I think this makes you invisible.	FESTE Not so, sir, I do care for something; but in my conscience, sir, I do not care for you. If that be to care for nothing*, sir, I would it would make you invisible.

Note: 'Nothing' – A common term in Elizabethan England used as a double entendre for female genitalia. , and as 'nothing' is not visible then it is invisible.

VIOLA (AS CESARIO) Aren't you Lady Olivia's fool?	VIOLA Art not thou the Lady Olivia's fool?
FESTE Indeed no, sir, the Lady Olivia is not foolish. She'll have no fool, sir, till she is married. And fools are to husbands as sprats are to herrings – one is just bigger. I am not her fool, merely her corrupter of words.	FESTE No indeed, sir, the Lady Olivia has no folly. She will keep no fool, sir, till she be married; and fools are as like husbands as pilchards are to herrings - the husband's the bigger. I am indeed not her fool, but her corrupter of words.*

Note: 'Corrupter of words' – a statement which is apt throughout the play and will be touched upon later. Feste is used as a vehicle for Shakespeare's clever wordplay.

VIOLA (AS CESARIO)
I also saw you recently at the palace of Count Orsino.

VIOLA
I saw thee late at the Count Orsino's.

FESTE
Foolery, sir, walks around the Earth like the sun, it shines everywhere. It would be a pity, sir, if the fool was not with your master as often as with my mistress. I think I saw your (*sarcastic*) 'clever self' there.

FESTE
Foolery, sir, does walk about the orb like the sun,* it shines everywhere. I would be sorry, sir, but the fool should be as oft with your master as with my mistress. I think I saw your wisdom* there.

**Note:* 'Like the Sun' - Back then, thanks to Ptolemy, astronomers believed the seven visible planets (including the Moon and the Sun) were carried around the Earth in invisible spheres, with an outer eighth sphere containing them and all the stars (the firmament). The whole system was contained in a ninth sphere, the Primum Mobile, itself contained within the Empyrean, the fastest moving sphere, revolving around the earth (the centre of the system) in twenty-four hours carrying the inner spheres with it. However, Copernicus had proved by 1543 that the earth revolved around the Sun, but the Church considered this heresy.*

'Wisdom' – he sarcastically calls Viola a fool.

VIOLA (AS CESARIO)
Well, if you poke fun at me, I'll stay no longer. (*having a sudden thought*) Wait…

VIOLA
Nay, and thou pass upon me, I'll no more with thee. Hold,

Note: 'Pass upon me' – a fencing expression. A pass is a thrust.

VIOLA RUMMAGES IN HER MONEY PURSE.

VIOLA (AS CESARIO) (CONT'D)
… here's something for your time.

VIOLA
...there's expenses for thee.

VIOLA (AS CESARIO) GIVES FESTE A COIN.

FESTE TAKES IT, MOCKINGLY STROKING THE SMOOTH SKIN OF VIOLA'S FACE.

FESTE
When he next has hair in stock, may God send you a beard.

FESTE
Now Jove, in his next commodity of hair, send thee a beard.*

**Trivia: 'Beard' is also theatre slang for an actor playing an adult male role (females were barred from acting).*

VIOLA (AS CESARIO)
Upon my word, I tell you, I desire one more than anything.
(*aside to audience*) Though I'd not want it to grow on my chin.
(*aloud*) Is your lady in?

VIOLA
By my troth, I'll tell thee, I am almost sick for one,
[Aside.] though I would not have it grow on my chin.*
[Aloud.] Is thy lady within?

**Note: 'Grow on my chin' – a double entendre – she is sick with desire for a man with a beard on his chin – Duke Orsini. The other meaning is hair growing on another part of her body. It depends on the emphasis on the word 'my' as to which meaning is inferred.*

FESTE INDICATES THE COIN IN HIS HAND, HINTING HE'D LIKE MORE.

FESTE
Wouldn't a '*pair*' of these breed, sir?

FESTE
Would not a pair of these have bred, sir?

VIOLA (AS CESARIO)
Yes, if kept together and put to good use.

VIOLA
Yes, being kept together and put to use.*

**Note: 'Put to use' – double meaning of gaining interest and breeding/copulating.*

FESTE POINTS AT THE COIN IN HIS HAND.

FESTE
Then I'd like to act as Lord Pandarus of Phrygia, sir, and bring a Cressida to this Troilus.

FESTE
I would play Lord Pandarus of Phrygia, sir, to bring a Cressida to this Troilus.*

**Note: Troilus and Cressida were brought together by Pandarus of Troy so they could become lovers. Cressida was a beggar and Troilus was a leper.*

VIOLA RUMMAGES IN HER MONEY PURSE AGAIN.

VIOLA (AS CESARIO)
I understand your meaning, sir. It is good begging.

VIOLA
I understand you, sir; 'tis well begged.

VIOLA PRODUCES ANOTHER COIN

FESTE TAKES THE COIN.

explain

FESTE	FESTE
It is no big deal I hope, sir, begging for a beggar – after all, Cressida was a beggar. My lady is in, sir. I will announce to them where you have come from. Who you are and what you want are out of my sphere - I could say 'element', but the word is overused.	The matter, I hope, is not great, sir, begging but a beggar - Cressida was a beggar. My lady is within, sir. I will conster* to them whence you come. Who you are and what you would are out of my welkin*; I might say `element', but the word is overworn.

**Note: 'Conster' – some editions replace this word with 'construe'. It is Feste using mock high-brow words. Conster is the old spelling for construe. It means to explain or interpret.*

'Welkin' – sky, heavens.

EXIT FESTE TO DELIVER THE MESSAGE.

VIOLA (AS CESARIO)	VIOLA
(*aside*) The fellow is clever enough to act the fool, and to do that well requires intelligence. He must observe the mood of those he jests to, the social standing of them, the occasion, and, like the untrained hawk, fly at every prey he sees. This is a profession requiring as much hard work as any wise man's occupation. *Folly shown wisely is the expert's tools,* *But wise men fooling badly, just look like fools.*	This fellow is wise enough to play the fool, And to do that well craves a kind of wit: He must observe their mood on whom he jests, The quality of persons, and the time, And, like the haggard*, check at every feather* That comes before his eye.* This is a practice As full of labour as a wise man's art; *For folly that he wisely shows is fit,* *But wise men, folly-fall'n, quite taint their wit.*

**Note: 'Haggard' – a young untrained hawk that chases anything in its sight, being easily distracted from its intended prey. Trainers would swing a lure in the air, called a 'feather', to train the bird. Another hawking reference, one of Shakespeare's most popular themes.*

ENTER SIR TOBY AND SIR ANDREW, BOTH THE WORSE FOR DRINK.

SIR TOBY BELCH	SIR TOBY BELCH
God be with you, gentleman.	Save you, gentleman.
VIOLA (AS CESARIO)	VIOLA
And you, sir.	And you, sir.
SIR ANDREW AGUECHEEK	SIR ANDREW AGUECHEEK
Dieu vous garde, monsieur.	Dieu vous garde, monsieur.*
VIOLA (AS CESARIO)	VIOLA
Et vous aussi, votre serviteur.	Et vous aussi; votre serviteur.*

**Note: Sir Andrew repeats Sir Toby's words in French. Viola replies in French, which translated means, "And you also, I am your servant".*

SIR ANDREW AGUECHEEK	SIR ANDREW AGUECHEEK
I hope, sir, you are, and I am yours.	I hope, sir, you are, and I am yours.

SIR TOBY PUTS ON DRUNKENLY SLURRED AIRS AND GRACES.

SIR TOBY BELCH Will you be making an entrance to the house? My niece is desirous you should enter, if your business is with her.	SIR TOBY BELCH Will you encounter the house? My niece is desirous you should enter, if your trade be to her.

VIOLA REPLIES IN NAUTICAL TERMS.

VIOLA (AS CESARIO) I am bound for your niece, sir. She is the destination of my voyage, I mean.	VIOLA I am bound to your niece, sir; I mean, she is the list of my voyage.
SIR TOBY BELCH Then taste your legs, sir, put them in motion.	SIR TOBY BELCH Taste your legs*, sir; put them to motion.
VIOLA (AS CESARIO) My legs 'under stand' me better, sir, than I understand what you mean by telling me to taste my legs.	VIOLA My legs do better understand* me, sir, than I understand what you mean by bidding me taste my legs.*

**Note: 'Understand' – stand under me, double meaning.*

Sir Toby refers to testing something by tasting it – taste test.

SIR TOBY BELCH I mean, to go in sir, to enter.	SIR TOBY BELCH I mean, to go, sir, to enter.
VIOLA (AS CESARIO) My gait and entrance will answer you, sir.	VIOLA I will answer you with gait and entrance.

**Note: 'Gait and entrance' walking and entering. A play on 'gate and doorway'.*

AS VIOLA STARTS WALKING SHE SEES OLIVIA AND MARIA APPROACHING THEM.

VIOLA (AS CESARIO) (CONT'D) But it seems we are anticipated.	VIOLA But we are prevented.

VIOLA ADDRESSES OLIVIA.

VIOLA (AS CESARIO) (CONT'D) Most excellent and accomplished lady, may the heavens rain sweet odours upon you!	VIOLA Most excellent accomplished lady, the heavens rain odours on you!
SIR ANDREW AGUECHEEK That youth's a good courtier, "Rain sweet odours" - very good.	SIR ANDREW AGUECHEEK That youth's a rare courtier. "Rain odours" - well.

VIOLA (AS CESARIO)
My message, lady, only has voice for your own most expectant and attendant ear.

VIOLA
My matter hath no voice, lady, but to your own most pregnant and vouchsafed ear.

SIR ANDREW AGUECHEEK
“Odours”, “expectant”, and “attendant” – I must remember to use all three of these.

SIR ANDREW AGUECHEEK
"Odours", "pregnant", and "vouchsafed" - I'll get 'em all three all ready.

OLIVIA
(*to others*) Close the garden gate, and leave me to my private hearing.

OLIVIA
Let the garden door be shut, and leave me to my hearing.

EXEUNT SIR TOBY, SIR ANDREW AND MARIA.

OLIVIA (CONT’D)
Give me your hand, sir.

OLIVIA
Give me your hand, sir.

ALTHOUGH OLIVIA OFFERS HER HAND, POSSIBLY AS AN EQUAL RATHER THAN AS A SUPERIOR RANK, VIOLA RESPECTFULLY KNEELS BEFORE HER, TAKING THE OFFERED HAND AND KISSING IT.

VIOLA (AS CESARIO)
I offer my humble service to you, madam.

VIOLA
My duty, madam, and most humble service.

OLIVIA
What is your name?

OLIVIA
What is your name?

VIOLA STANDS.

VIOLA (AS CESARIO)
Cesario is the name of your servant, fair princess.

VIOLA
Cesario is your servant's* name, fair princess.

**Note: ‘Servant’ – also a term used in gallantry by suitors to a lady whose love they sought, emphasised by calling her ‘fair princess’ as if from the days of knights in shining armour.*

VIOLA BOWS DRAMATICALLY.

OLIVIA
My servant, sir? It’s a sad world where false fawning is considered a compliment. You’re the servant of Count Orsino, young man.

OLIVIA
My servant, sir? 'Twas never merry world
Since lowly feigning was called compliment.
Y'are servant to the Count Orsino, youth.

VIOLA (AS CESARIO)
And he is yours, and all that is his is yours. Your servant’s servant is your servant, madam.

VIOLA
And he is yours, and his must needs be yours:
Your servant's servant is your servant, madam.

OLIVIA
As for him, I don't think about him, and as for his thoughts, I wish they were blank pages rather than filled with me.

OLIVIA
For him, I think not on him; for his thoughts,
Would they were blanks rather than filled with me.

VIOLA (AS CESARIO)
Madam, I come on his behalf to tempt your gentle thoughts towards him.

VIOLA
Madam, I come to whet your gentle thoughts
On his behalf.

OLIVIA
Oh, please don't, I beg of you. I asked you never to speak on his behalf again. But if you must make another plea, I would rather hear you asking it than listen to angelic music.

OLIVIA
O, by your leave, I pray you.
I bade you never speak again of him;
But, would you undertake another suit,
I had rather hear you to solicit that
Than music from the spheres.*

**Note: 'Olivia is hinting she would rather hear Viola pleading for herself than for Orsino.*

VIOLA (AS CESARIO)
Dear lady…

VIOLA
Dear lady -

OLIVIA
(*interrupting*) Wait, pardon my interruption, but, after your last enchanting visit here, I sent a ring after you. In doing so I abused myself, and my servant, and, I fear, I abused you as well. It is under your harsh judgement I must sit for forcing the ring on you in such a shameful manner when you knew it was not yours. What can you think of me?

OLIVIA
Give me leave, beseech you. I did send,
After the last enchantment you did here,
A ring in chase of you. So did I abuse
Myself, my servant, and, I fear me, you.
Under your hard construction must I sit,
To force that on you in a shameful cunning
Which you knew none of yours. What might you think?

OLIVIA BLUSHES, EMBARRASSED, THEN CONTINUES.

OLIVIA (CONT'D)
I've put my honour at stake, and you've probably mocked it with all the malicious thoughts a cruel heart could imagine. To someone of your understanding enough has been shown. My bosom no longer conceals my heart, it is on open view beneath sheer linen. So, let me hear your thoughts.

OLIVIA
Have you not set mine honour at the stake*,
And baited it with all th' unmuzzled thoughts*
That tyrannous heart can think? To one of your receiving
Enough is shown: a cypress*, not a bosom,
Hides my heart. So, let me hear you speak.

**Note: 'At the stake' – another bear-baiting reference. The bear is chained to the stake and 'unmuzzled' dogs are set upon it, 'baiting' it. Olivia suggests she was the poor bear and the uncontrolled malicious thoughts were the dogs attacking her. Shakespeare has twisted the saying "my honour is at stake". A stake is a wager at risk of being lost, also a wooden pole.*

'Cypress' – a thin transparent material. She is revealing her heart, hiding nothing, and attempting to seduce Viola (as Cesario) with the imagery.

VIOLA (AS CESARIO)
I feel pity for you.

OLIVIA
That's a step towards love.

VIOLA (AS CESARIO)
No, not even a small one - it's a common fact that we often pity our enemies.

VIOLA
I pity you.

OLIVIA
That's a degree to love.

VIOLA
No, not a grize*; for 'tis a vulgar proof
That very oft we pity enemies.

**Note: 'Grize', or 'grece' in some editions – a small step often leading up to a throne or altar.*

VIOLA HANDS THE RING BACK TO OLIVIA.

OLIVIA
In that case, I think it is time to relax and smile again. Oh, world, the stubborn pride of the poor people! Anyway, if I am to be hunted, how much better to fall before a lion than a wolf.

OLIVIA
Why, then methinks 'tis time to smile again.
O world, how apt the poor are to be proud!
If one should be a prey, how much the better
To fall before the lion than the wolf.*

**Note: 'Smile again' – Now Olivia knows Viola does not return her love and instead of being angry with her for giving the ring, Viola only pities her, Olivia can stop worrying.*

'Fall before the lion…' – she is peeved that the lowly 'poor' messenger has rejected her advances. She says it is better anyway to be pursued by the lion (Orsino) than the wolf (Viola). The double innuendo of 'fall before' chosen because it has sexual connotations as well as submitting to the advances.

A CLOCK STRIKES THE HOUR.

OLIVIA (CONT'D)
The clock rebukes me for wasting my time. Don't be afraid, dear youth, I will not have you now. Though when you've reached maturity your wife will likely find in you a complete man.

OLIVIA
The clock upbraids me with the waste of time.*
Be not afraid, good youth, I will not have you;*
And yet, when wit and youth is come to harvest,
Your wife* is like to reap a proper man.

**Note: 'Waste of time' – in pursuing Viola.*

'Have you' – I will not pursue/marry you, again she uses sexually charged words.

'Your wife' – Olivia still hopes this will be herself.

OLIVIA DISMISSES VIOLA, POINTING IN A WESTWARD DIRECTION.

OLIVIA (CONT'D)
Your destination lies due west.

OLIVIA
There lies your way, due west.

VIOLA (AS CESARIO)	VIOLA
Then westward ho! May the grace of heaven and inner peace be with your ladyship. (*she bows*) You've nothing, my lady, for my lord through me?	Then westward ho!* Grace and good disposition attend your ladyship. You'll nothing*, madam, to my lord by me?

Note: 'Westward ho' – the cry of the River Thames ferrymen to passengers for boats heading west towards the royal court at Westminster from the Globe theatre. Those heading east cried, "Eastward ho!"

Not to be confused with the village Westwood Ho! in Devon. It was also the title of a famous book by Charles Kingsley about the heroic adventures of famous Elizabethan explorers such as Drake and Raleigh.

Note the use of the word 'nothing' again.

Old woodcut drawing of a Thames ferry

OLIVIA	OLIVIA
Wait!	Stay!

OLIVIA PAUSES DRAMATICALLY (INDICATED BY THE SINGLE WORDED LINE).

OLIVIA (CONT'D)	OLIVIA
I beg you, tell me what you really think of me.	I prithee tell me what thou think'st of me.

Note: 'Thou' – Olivia uses the familiar address of 'thou' rather than the formal 'you' she has used up till now.

VIOLA (AS CESARIO)	VIOLA
That you are mistaken in thinking what you think.	That you do think you are not what you are.*

Note: Viola is talking in riddles. She is not what Olivia thinks she is, Olivia is mistaken in thinking Viola is male and was rejected because Viola believes he is beneath her in status. Also implied is that Olivia is mistaken about Orsino not being desirable.

OLIVIA	OLIVIA
If I am mistaken, then I think the same applies to you.	If I think so, I think the same of you.*

Note: Olivia hopes Viola may be of more noble birth and could be convinced to love her.

VIOLA (AS CESARIO)	VIOLA
Then you think correctly. I am not what I am.	Then think you right: I am not what I am.
OLIVIA	OLIVIA
I wish you were the way I'd have you be.	I would you were as I would have you be.*

Note: 'Have you be' – in love with her. 'Have you' is yet another innuendo.

VIOLA (AS CESARIO)
Would I be better, madam, than I am now? I hope so, as right now you are making a fool of me.

VIOLA
Would it be better, madam, than I am?
I wish it might, for now I am your fool.*

**Note: 'I am your fool' – Olivia tells Viola to go, then tells her to stay, says she does not love Viola, then asks Viola whether she could love Olivia.*

THEY END THE SCENE BY SPEAKING IN RHYME.

OLIVIA
(*aside*) Oh, how scorn can look so beautiful in the contempt and anger of his voice!
A murderer's guilt shows less in bright light
Than love one keeps hidden by the dark night.

(to Viola) Cesario, now, by the roses of spring,
By innocence, honour, truth, everything,
I love you so much that, despite all my pride,
No rhyme nor reason can my passion hide.
Don't give me reasons why I should desist
From my pursuit, there's no need to resist.
Instead please allow your reason's arrest:
Love asked for's good, but giv'n unasked is best.

OLIVIA
[Aside.] O, what a deal of scorn looks beautiful
In the contempt and anger of his lip!
A murd'rous guilt shows not itself more soon
Than love that would seem hid. Love's night is noon.

[To VIOLA.] Cesario, by the roses of the spring,
By maidhood, honour, truth, and everything,
I love thee so that, maugre all thy pride,
Nor wit nor reason can my passion hide.
Do not extort thy reasons from this clause,
For that I woo, thou therefore hast no cause;
But rather reason thus with reason fetter:
Love sought is good, but given unsought is better.

VIOLA (AS CESARIO)
I swear by my innocence and my youth,
In my heart and bosom, there's just one truth,
That no woman has, nor ever will be
Mistress of my heart, except only me.
And so adieu, madam, and never more
Will I bring my master's tears to your door.

VIOLA
By innocence I swear, and by my youth,
I have one heart, one bosom, and one truth,
And that no woman has; nor never none
Shall mistress be of it, save I alone.
And so adieu, good madam. Never more
Will I my master's tears to you deplore.

OLIVIA
But do come again, for perhaps you may move
This heart which abhors him to liking his love.

OLIVIA
*Yet come again; for thou perhaps mayst move**
That heart which now abhors to like his love.

**Note: 'Love' rhymed with 'move' back then. Shakespeare often rhymed love with words (such as move and prove) which to us seem a bad rhyme, but then were a perfect rhyme.*

Once again Olivia really means Viola (as Cesario) when she refers to Orsino's love.

EXEUNT.

ACT III SCENE II

A ROOM IN OLIVIA'S HOUSE.

ENTER SIR ANDREW, PURSUED BY SIR TOBY AND FABIAN, ALL ARGUING.

SIR ANDREW AGUECHEEK
Indeed, no, I'll not stay a moment longer.

SIR ANDREW AGUECHEEK
No, faith, I'll not stay a jot longer.

SIR TOBY BELCH
Your reason, dear sourpuss, give your reason.

SIR TOBY BELCH
Thy reason, dear venom, give thy reason.

FABIAN
You must give us your reason, Sir Andrew.

FABIAN
You must needs yield your reason, Sir Andrew.

SIR ANDREW STOPS AND TURNS. SIR TOBY AND FABIAN BUMP INTO HIM.

SIR ANDREW AGUECHEEK
Because, I saw your niece offer more favours to the Count's serving man than she ever offered me. I saw them together in the garden.

SIR ANDREW AGUECHEEK
Marry, I saw your niece do more favours to the count's* servingman than ever she bestowed upon me. I saw't i'th orchard*. — garden

**Note: 'Count's' - The way this word is delivered could be as an expletive – a substitute for a similar sounding swear word.*

'Orchard' – garden (or yard in North America).

SIR TOBY BELCH
Did she see you though, old boy? Tell me that.

SIR TOBY BELCH
Did she see thee the while, old boy? - tell me that.

SIR ANDREW AGUECHEEK
As plain as I see you now.

SIR ANDREW AGUECHEEK
As plain as I see you now.

FABIAN
This is a strong indication of her love for you.

FABIAN
This was a great argument of love in her toward you.

SIR ANDREW AGUECHEEK
Strewth! Are you making an ass of me?

SIR ANDREW AGUECHEEK
'Slight! - will you make an ass o' me?

FABIAN
I will prove my claim, sir, enough to convince a grand jury.

FABIAN
I will prove it legitimate, sir, upon the oaths of judgment and reason.

SIR TOBY BELCH
And a grand jury has been good enough judgement since before Noah was a sailor.

SIR TOBY BELCH
And they have been grand-jurymen since before Noah was a sailor.

NOAH

FABIAN

She showed her favour to the youth while you watched only to make you jealous, to awaken your sleeping courage, to put fire in your heart and awaken your passion. You should have accosted her there and then, and used witty lines she'd not heard before, you should have struck the youth speechless. This was expected of you, and you let her down. You let time wash the gilt off this golden opportunity, and you have now sailed north of the lady's affection, and there you will hang, like an icicle on a Dutchman's beard unless you rescue it by some praiseworthy action of either valour or strategic policy.

FABIAN

She did show favour to the youth in your sight only to exasperate you, to awake your dormouse valour, to put fire in your heart and brimstone in your liver*. You should then have accosted her*, and with some excellent jests, fire-new from the mint,* you should have banged the youth into dumbness. This was looked for at your hand, and this was balked. The double gilt of this opportunity you let time wash off, and you are now sailed into the north of my lady's opinion, where you will hang like an icicle on a Dutchman's beard unless you do redeem it by some laudable attempt either of valour or policy.

**Note: 'Liver' – it was believed the liver was the source of passion and bravery.*

'Accosted her' – the audience will likely remember these words used by Sir Toby earlier.

'Fire new from the mint' – freshly minted – like a new penny.

'Dutchman's beard' – a reference to the arctic expedition in 1596 of explorer Willem Barents which cost him his life there in 1597.

SIR ANDREW AGUECHEEK

If it has to be one or the other then it must be with valour, as I hate policy. I'd rather be a Puritan than a politician.

SIR ANDREW AGUECHEEK

And't be any way, it must be with valour; for policy I hate. I had as lief be a Brownist as a politician.

SIR TOBY BELCH

Well then, do as I say, and base your fortunes on valour. Let me see you challenge the count's young messenger to a fight. Hurt him in eleven places. My niece will hear of it, and be assured, there is no matchmaker in the world more powerful in a man's favour with women than a report of valour.

SIR TOBY BELCH

Why then, build me thy fortunes upon the basis of valour. Challenge me the count's youth to fight with him; hurt him in eleven places*. My niece shall take note of it; and assure thyself, there is no love-broker in the world can more prevail in man's commendation with woman than report of valour.

**Note: 'Hurt him in eleven places' - refers to the ten body areas Italian fencing masters aimed their cuts to, and the direction of the cut. The additional point thrust to the centre of the target, the opponent's navel, being the eleventh (like getting a bullseye).*

The cuts shown on the right are from a 1536 illustration.

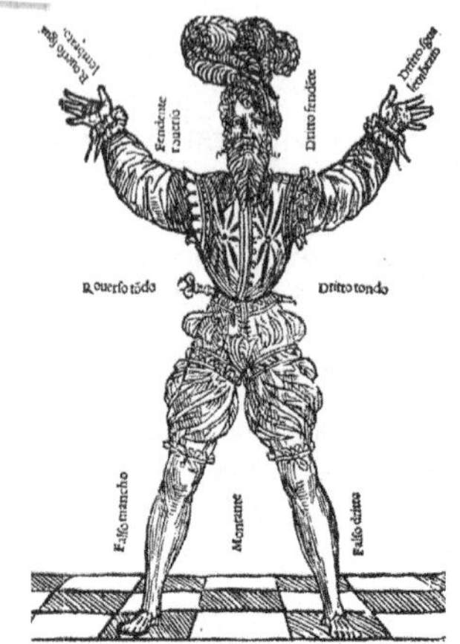

FABIAN
This is the only way, Sir Andrew.

SIR ANDREW AGUECHEEK
Would either of you deliver my challenge to him?

SIR TOBY BELCH
Go and write it in a strictly formal manner, be curt and to the point. It doesn't have to be clever, as long as it is eloquent and original. Taunt him with the power of the written word. If you address him in a friendly manner no more than three times, that's acceptable, and put down as many lies as will lie on a sheet of paper, even if that sheet is big enough for the biggest bed in England, write them down. Get going. Let there be spirit in your ink, even though you'll be writing with a white feather, don't worry about that. Now, go to it.

FABIAN
There is no way but this, Sir Andrew.

SIR ANDREW AGUECHEEK
Will either of you bear me a challenge to him?

SIR TOBY BELCH
Go, write it in a martial hand; be curst and brief. It is no matter how witty, so it be eloquent and full of invention. Taunt him with the licence of ink. If thou thou'st him some thrice, it shall not be amiss; and as many lies as will lie in thy sheet of paper, although the sheet were big enough for the bed of Ware* in England, set 'em down. Go, about it. Let there be gall enough in thy ink, though thou write with a goose-pen, no matter. About it.

**Note: 'Bed of Ware' – the largest known bed in England. An Elizabethan bed from an inn in Ware which measures over 3 square metres (32 sq feet). Rumour had it that it was big enough for 12 people. It can be viewed today in the Victoria and Albert Museum, London.*

SIR ANDREW AGUECHEEK
Where can I find you later?

SIR TOBY BELCH
We'll collect you from your room. Go!

SIR ANDREW AGUECHEEK
Where shall I find you?

SIR TOBY BELCH
We'll call thee at the cubiculo.* Go.

**Note: 'Cubiculo' – latin for bedroom.*

EXIT SIR ANDREW.

FABIAN
He's a dear little puppet to you, Sir Toby.

SIR TOBY BELCH
I have been dear to him, man, by some two thousand pounds or more.

FABIAN
This is a dear manikin to you, Sir Toby.

SIR TOBY BELCH
I have been dear to him, lad, some two thousand* strong or so.

**Note: 'Two thousand' – in those days was a very large sum of money.*

FABIAN
We'll have quite some letter from him, but you'll not deliver it, I trust?

FABIAN
We shall have a rare letter from him; but you'll not deliver't.

SIR TOBY BELCH
Never trust me again if I don't, and I'll push the youth for an answer, as I think not even a carriage with four horses could drive them together. As for Sir Andrew, if he was to be opened up and you found enough blood in his liver to drown a flea, I'll eat the rest of his organs.

SIR TOBY BELCH
Never trust me then; and by all means stir on the youth to an answer. I think oxen and wainropes cannot hale them together. For Andrew, if he were opened and you find so much blood in his liver* as will clog the foot of a flea, I'll eat the rest of th' anatomy.

**Note: 'Liver' – it was believed the liver produced the blood in the body, so it was the source of strength and bravery (hence lily-livered for a coward), the heart was thought to control emotions of love (still to this day).*

FABIAN
And his opponent, the youth, has in his face no look of great cruelty.

FABIAN
And his opposite, the youth, bears in his visage no great presage of cruelty.

ENTER MARIA.

SIR TOBY BELCH
Look, here comes the smallest of the smallest birds.

SIR TOBY BELCH
Look where the youngest wren* of nine comes.

**Note: 'Youngest wren' – one of the smallest of birds, and the last hatched bird was in folklore deemed to be the smallest, and the smallest of nine made this very tiny.*

MARIA
If you want to split your sides laughing in amusement, follow me. That stupid bird Malvolio has turned heathen, a true renegade, for there is no Christian could hope for salvation from such gross acts of behaviour. He's in yellow tights!

MARIA
If you desire the spleen*, and will laugh yourselves into stitches*, follow me. Yond gull Malvolio is turned heathen, a very renegado; for there is no Christian that means to be saved by believing rightly can ever believe such impossible passages of grossness. He's in yellow stockings.

**Note: 'Spleen' – Amusing fun – the spleen was believed to be the source of laughter.*

'Stitches' – the old saying 'you will split your sides laughing' evolved into 'you'll be in stitches' – meaning after your sides are split you will need stitches to repair them.

SIR TOBY BELCH
Are they cross-gartered?

MARIA
Most horrendously, like a religious zealot who is so obsessed his classroom is in a church.

SIR TOBY BELCH
And cross-gartered?

MARIA
Most villainously, like a pedant that keeps a school i'th church.*

Note: 'Pedant' – this is possibly another dig by Shakespeare at the Puritans at the time who were pedantic about religious practices and social behaviour. They were not popular or fashionable.

THE TWO MEN LAUGH RAUCOUSLY AT THIS.

MARIA (CONT)
I have stalked him like a serial killer. He has obeyed every detail of the letter I dropped in order to undo him. His smile screws his face up with more lines than the new map of the Caribbean islands. You've not seen anything like it. I can hardly stop myself throwing things at him. I know my lady will beat him, and if she does he'll only smile and take it as a sign of her affection.

MARIA
I have dogged him like his murderer. He does obey every point of the letter that I dropped to betray him: he does smile his face into more lines than is in the new map* with the augmentation of the Indies. You have not seen such a thing as 'tis. I can hardly forbear hurling things at him. I know my lady will strike him; if she do, he'll smile and take't for a great favour.

SIR TOBY BELCH
Come, take us, take us to where he is.

SIR TOBY BELCH
Come bring us, bring us where he is.

THEY HURRY AWAY FOLLOWING MARIA.

**Note: 'New map' – referring to a new map of the time found in Haylut's Voyages (1589) where the West Indies (Caribbean) were drawn in greater detail than in any previous map.*

Originally inhabited by Arawak and Carib Indians, the islands were visited by Columbus in 1492 and named by him in the belief that he had reached the west coast of India. The islands now consist of independent states and British, French, Dutch, and US dependencies.

Map from Haylut's Voyages 1589

ACT III SCENE III

A STREET IN ILLYRIA.

ENTER SEBASTIAN AND ANTONIO.

THEY ARE WALKING FROM THE SHORE TOWARDS THE TOWN.

SEBASTIAN
By choice I would not have put you to all this trouble, but since you seem to find pleasure in your troubles, I'll chastise you no longer.

SEBASTIAN
I would not by my will have troubled you;
But since you make your pleasure of your pains,
I will no further chide you.

ANTONIO
I could not stay behind. My desire to help is keener than any sharpened blade and urges me on. It's not just my desire to be with you – though that alone is enough for me to undertake a longer journey – but also the worry of what may befall your travels in this unfamiliar country which can be rough and inhospitable to a stranger with no friend to guide them. I willingly follow you out of love, combined with fears for your safety.

ANTONIO
I could not stay behind you. My desire,
More sharp than filed steel, did spur me forth;
And not all love to see you - though so much
As might have drawn one to a longer voyage -
But jealousy what might befall your travel,
Being skilless in these parts, which to a stranger,
Unguided and unfriended, often prove
Rough and unhospitable. My willing love*
The rather by these arguments of fear
Set forth in your pursuit.

**Note: 'Love' – respect, like. Love was used often in Elizabethan English to suggest a strong liking, not a physical attraction. Such as we would say today, "I would love an ice cream".*

SEBASTIAN
My dear, kind Antonio, I can give no other answer than my thanks, more thanks, and thanks ever after. Often good turns are palmed off with mere words which hold no monetary value, but if my wealth were as large as my conscience you'd be much more handsomely rewarded.
- What shall we do? Shall we see what sights this town has to offer?

SEBASTIAN
My kind Antonio,
I can no other answer make but thanks,
And thanks, [and ever thanks;]* and oft good turns
Are shuffled off with such uncurrent pay;
But were my worth, as is my conscience, firm,
You should find better dealing. What's to do?
Shall we go see the relics of this town?

**Note: 'And ever thanks' – these words were not in the original texts. As the line's meter and meaning make no sense with the omission of these words it is presumed to have been a printer's error due to the repetition of so many 'thanks' and modern editions now include them.*

ANTONIO
Tomorrow, sir. First, we'd best find you some lodgings.

ANTONIO
Tomorrow, sir; best first go see your lodging.

SEBASTIAN
I am not tired, and the day is young. I beg you, let's feast our eyes on the old monuments and historic places this town is famed for.

SEBASTIAN
I am not weary, and 'tis long to night.
I pray you, let us satisfy our eyes
With the memorials and the things of fame
That do renown this city.

ANTONIO
Forgive me, but walking these streets is not without danger for me. You see, I once served in a sea battle against the Count's warships, I played such a notable part in it that if I were captured here there would be no hope for me.

ANTONIO
Would you'd pardon me:
I do not without danger walk these streets.
Once in a sea-fight* 'gainst the Count* his galleys*
I did some service; of such note, indeed,
That were I ta'en here it would scarce be answered.

Note: 'Sea-fight' – suggesting Antonio had been a pirate.

'Count' – Duke (or Count) Orsino.

'Galleys' – Mediterranean naval ships.

Mediterranean Galley

SEBASTIAN
Because you killed a lot of his people?

SEBASTIAN
Belike you slew great number of his people.

ANTONIO
The offence is not so bloody in nature, though the circumstances of the argument may well have led to bloodshed. It could have been resolved by returning what we stole from them, which, to keep trade lines open most of my country did. Only I objected, and because of this, if I were captured here I would pay dearly.

ANTONIO
Th' offence is not of such a bloody nature,
Albeit the quality of the time and quarrel
Might well have given us bloody argument.
It might have since been answered in repaying
What we took from them, which, for traffic's sake,
Most of our city did. Only myself stood out;
For which, if I be lapsed in this place,
I shall pay dear.

SEBASTIAN
Don't walk so openly in public then.

SEBASTIAN
Do not then walk too open.

ANTONIO
It would not be good for me. Wait, sir, here's my purse.

ANTONIO
It doth not fit me. Hold, sir, here's my purse.

ANTONIO HANDS SEBASTIAN A LEATHER PURSE CONTAINING MONEY.

ANTONIO (CONT'D) In the southern suburbs, the Elephant Inn is the best place to lodge, I'll order food for us there. After you've passed the time feeding your knowledge viewing the sights of the town you can meet me there	ANTONIO In the south suburbs at the Elephant* Is best to lodge - I will bespeak our diet, Whiles you beguile the time and feed your knowledge With viewing of the town - there shall you have me.

**Note: 'Elephant' – an inn by this name stood close to the Globe Theatre which was situated on the south bank of the river in the south suburbs of London.*

SEBASTIAN Why should I have your purse?	SEBASTIAN Why I your purse?
ANTONIO Perhaps your gaze will fall upon some trinket you'd like to purchase. I suspect your cash reserves are insufficient for souvenir markets.	ANTONIO Haply your eye shall light upon some toy You have desire to purchase; and your store I think is not for idle markets, sir.
SEBASTIAN I'll be your purse-bearer and leave you for an hour.	SEBASTIAN I'll be your purse-bearer and leave you for An hour.
ANTONIO Meet me at the Elephant.	ANTONIO To th' Elephant.
SEBASTIAN I will remember.	SEBASTIAN I do remember.

THEY EXIT IN DIFFERENT DIRECTIONS.

ACT III SCENE IV

OLIVIA'S GARDEN.

ENTER OLIVIA AND MARIA. OLIVIA IS DEEP IN THOUGHT, MARIA STANDS BY THE DOOR IN ATTENDANCE.

Note: This is a long scene.

OLIVIA (*aside*) I have sent for him. Suppose he says he'll come? What feast shall I prepare for him? What gift shall I give him? Youth is more often won over by gifts than kind words or promises. – I am talking too loudly. (*to Maria*) Where's Malvolio?	OLIVIA [*Aside.*] I have sent after him; he says he'll come. How shall I feast him? What bestow of him? For youth is bought more oft than begged or borrowed.* I speak too loud. [*To Maria.*] Where's Malvolio?

**Note: 'Begged or borrowed' – twisting the proverb "better to buy than beg or borrow"*

EXIT MARIA TO CALL MALVOLIO.

OLIVIA (*aside*) He is serious and obliging, he is well suited to be my servant, what with my mixed fortunes. (*aloud exasperated*) Where <u>is</u> Malviolio?	OLIVIA [*Aside.*] He is sad and civil, And suits well for a servant with my fortunes. Where is Malvolio?

RE-ENTER MARIA.

MARIA He's coming, madam, but he's behaving very strangely. I'm sure he's possessed, madam.	MARIA He's coming, madam, but in very strange manner. He is sure possessed,* madam.

**Note: 'Possessed' – taken over by a demon spirit or the Devil himself.*

OLIVIA Why? What's happened? Is he ranting and raving?	OLIVIA Why, what's the matter? Does he rave?

MARIA
(*suppressing giggles*) No, madam, but he won't stop smiling. It would be best if your ladyship has someone with you if he does come, the man has surely gone weak in the head.

MARIA
No, madam, he does nothing but smile. Your ladyship were best to have some guard about you if he come, for sure the man is tainted in's wits.

OLIVIA
Go tell him to hurry up.

OLIVIA
Go call him hither.

EXIT MARIA, SUPPRESSING HER LAUGHTER.

OLIVIA (CONT'D)
(*aside*) I'm as mad as he is, if sad madness and happy madness are equals.

OLIVIA
I am as mad as he,
If sad and merry madness equal be.

RE-ENTER MARIA PUSHING MALVOLIO INTO THE ROOM. HE WEARS CROSS-GARTERED YELLOW TIGHTS AND IS SMILING GROTESQUELY.

OLIVIA (CONT'D)
What's the matter, Malvolio?

OLIVIA
How now, Malvolio?

MALVOLIO
(*smiling and winking*) Sweet lady, ha, ha, ha!

MALVOLIO
Sweet lady, ho, ho!

OLIVIA
Why are you smiling? I sent for you on a serious matter.

OLIVIA
Smil'st thou? I sent for thee upon a sad* occasion.

**Note: 'Sad' - Olivia means serious, Malvolio takes the meaning to be unhappy.*

MALVOLIO
Serious, lady? I could easily be serious - this cross-gartering does obstruct blood flow somewhat, but so what? If it is pleasing to the eye of someone…

MALVOLIO
Sad, lady? I could be sad: this does make some obstruction in the blood, this cross-gartering, but what of that? If it please the eye of one -

MALVOLIO LOOKS DIRECTLY AT OLIVIA WITH A KNOWING WINK.

MALVOLIO (CONT'D)
…that is enough for me, as the love ballad says so accurately, "*Please one, and please all*".

MALVOLIO
- it is with me as the very true sonnet is, "*Please one and please all*"*.

**Note: 'Please one and please all' – a line taken from a ballad of the time, which the audience would have known had a bawdy meaning. The song was about pleasing women sexually. Malvolio may sing the phrase.*

MALVOLIO BLOWS A KISS TO A CONFUSED OLIVIA.

OLIVIA Why are you behaving like this, man? What's the matter with you?	OLIVIA Why, how dost thou, man? What is the matter with thee?
MALVOLIO I don't have black thoughts, even though I've yellow legs. (*laughs*) It *did* fall into his hands (*winks*), and orders will be carried out. (*slyly*) I think we recognise the handwriting. (*winks*)	MALVOLIO Not black in my mind, though yellow in my legs. It did come to his hands*, and commands shall be executed. I think we do know the sweet Roman hand.

**Note: 'Come to his hands' – he means the letter is in his possession.*

OLIVIA (*concerned*) Would you like to go to bed, Malvolio?	OLIVIA Wilt thou go to bed, Malvolio?
MALVOLIO To bed?	MALVOLIO To bed?

MALVOLIO BLOWS EXCITED KISSES HAVING TAKEN COMPLETELY THE WRONG MEANING IN OLIVIA'S STATEMENT. SHE MEANS HE SHOULD HAVE A LIE DOWN TO RECOVER.

MALVOLIO (CONT'D) Yes, sweetheart, and I'll join you.	MALVOLIO Ay, sweetheart, and I'll come to thee.

MALVOLIO'S SMILE IS NOW OF GROTESQUE PROPORTIONS.

OLIVIA God have mercy on you! Why do you smile so absurdly, and blow kisses so often?	OLIVIA God comfort thee! Why dost thou smile so, and kiss thy hand so oft?
MARIA Are you alright, Malvolio?	MARIA How do you, Malvolio?
MALVOLIO (*to Maria*) Me answer you? (*sarcastic*) Do nightingales answer crows?	MALVOLIO At your request? Yes, nightingales answer daws.*

**Note: 'Answer daws' – he sarcastically reminds Maria that he is above her in status. The prized sweet singing nightingale does not answer the stupid noisy jackdaw.*

MARIA Why do you behave with such ridiculous impertinence before my lady?	MARIA Why appear you with this ridiculous boldness before my lady?

MALVOLIO IGNORES MARIA SCORNFULLY AND ADRESSES OLIVIA.

MALVOLIO (*to Olivia*) "*Be not afraid of greatness*" – it was aptly written.	MALVOLIO "Be not afraid of greatness" -'twas well writ.
OLIVIA What do you mean by that, Malvolio?	OLIVIA What mean'st thou by that, Malvolio?
MALVOLIO "*Some are born great*"...	MALVOLIO *"Some are born great" -*
OLIVIA What?	OLIVIA Ha?
MALVOLIO "*Some achieve greatness*"...	MALVOLIO *"Some achieve greatness" -*
OLIVIA What are you saying?	OLIVIA What sayst thou?
MALVOLIO "*And some have greatness thrust upon them.*"	MALVOLIO *"And some have greatness thrust upon them."*
OLIVIA Heaven help you to your senses!	OLIVIA Heaven restore thee!
MALVOLIO "*Remember who praised your yellow tights.*"	MALVOLIO *"Remember who commended thy yellow stockings."*
OLIVIA My yellow tights?	OLIVIA Thy yellow stockings?
MALVOLIO "*And wished to see you cross-gartered.*"	MALVOLIO *"And wished to see thee cross-gartered."*
OLIVIA Cross gartered?	OLIVIA Cross-gartered?
MALVOLIO "*So, you can have it all if you want it.*"	MALVOLIO *"Go to, thou art made if thou* desir'st to be so."*
OLIVIA I can have it all?	OLIVIA Am I made?

**Note: 'Thou' – Olivia is offended by Malvolio addressing her with the familiar term 'thou' which is informal and used for friends of equals or those beneath you in social status, and also offended by thinking Malvolio is telling her she can have what she already has.*

MALVOLIO "*If not, stay a steward forever.*"	MALVOLIO *"If not, let me see thee a servant still."*

OLIVIA Why, this is complete midsummer madness.	OLIVIA Why, this is very midsummer madness.

ENTER A SERVANT.

SERVANT Madam, the young gentleman from the Count Orsino has returned. I could hardly hold him back. He wishes to see your ladyship.	SERVANT Madam, the young gentleman of the Count Orsino's is returned; I could hardly entreat him back. He attends your ladyship's pleasure.
OLIVIA I'll come to him.	OLIVIA I'll come to him.

OLIVIA WAVES THE SERVANT AWAY AND HE LEAVES.

OLIVIA (CONT'D) Good Maria, make sure this fellow is looked after. (*she indicates Malvolio*). Where's my cousin Toby? Let some of my people take special care of him. I'd rather lose half my dowry than see harm come to him.	OLIVIA Good Maria, let this fellow be looked to. Where's my cousin Toby? Let some of my people have a special care of him. I would not have him miscarry for the half of my dowry.

EXIT OLIVIA ONE WAY, AND MARIA WITH SERVANTS ANOTHER WAY, LEAVING MALVOLIO ALONE.

MALVOLIO (*aside*) Ah ha! So you begin to understand me now? No less a man than Sir Toby to look after me! This agrees exactly with the letter. She sends for him on purpose so I can be stubborn with him, just as she urges in her letter.	MALVOLIO O ho, do you come near me now? No worse man than Sir Toby to look to me! This concurs directly with the letter. She sends him on purpose that I may appear stubborn to him, for she incites me to that in the letter.

MALVOLIO TAKES OUT THE LETTER AND READS IT.

MALVOLIO (CONT'D) (*reads*) "*Cast off your humble demeaner*," she says, "*antagonise a kinsman and be surly with servants, let your tongue ring out with political arguments, adopt the role of one above others*". And she then sets down the manner in which it should be done – with a stern face, a noble bearing, slow of speech, clothed as a distinguished gentleman – and so forth.	MALVOLIO "*Cast thy humble slough*," says she, "*be opposite with a kinsman, surly with servants; let thy tongue tang with arguments of state; put thyself into the trick of singularity*"; and consequently sets down the manner how, as: a sad face, a reverend carriage, a slow tongue, in the habit of some sir of note, and so forth.

MALVOLIO LOOKS UP FROM THE LETTER.

MALVOLIO (CONT'D)
(*aside*) I have snared her. But it is God's doing, and may God make me thankful. And when she left just now she said, "*Make sure this fellow is looked after*". 'Fellow', not 'Malvolio', not as my role of steward, but as 'fellow'. Why, everything falls into place, not the smallest grain of doubt, not even a doubt of a doubt, no obstacle, no unexpected or difficult circumstance stands in the way. What more can be said? Nothing can come between me and the fulfilment of my hopes. Well, God, not I, is behind this, and he is to be thanked.

MALVOLIO
I have limed* her; but it is Jove's doing, and Jove make me thankful. And when she went away now, "*Let this fellow be looked to*". `*Fellow*', not `*Malvolio*', nor after my degree, but `*fellow*'. Why, everything adheres together that no dram of a scruple, no scruple of a scruple, no obstacle, no incredulous or unsafe circumstance - what can be said? Nothing that can be can come between me and the full prospect of my hopes. Well, Jove, not I, is the doer of this, and he is to be thanked.

**Note: 'Lime' – a trap for small birds. Sticky birdlime is smeared on branches.*

RE-ENTER MARIA, WITH SIR TOBY AND FABIAN.

MALVOLIO HURRIEDLY PUTS THE LETTER AWAY.

SIR TOBY BELCH
Where is he, in the name of all that's holy? If all the devils in hell have invaded him, and he's possessed by Satan himself, I'll still speak with him.

SIR TOBY BELCH
Which way is he, in the name of sanctity? If all the devils of hell be drawn in little, and Legion* himself possessed him, yet I'll speak to him.

**Note: 'Legion' – reference to Jesus Christ curing a man possessed by devils. "For Christ said unto him, Come out of the man you unclean spirit. And he asked him, What is your name? And he answered, My name is Legion: for we are many" (after a Roman legion which comprised of roughly 6,000 men).*

FABIAN
(*pointing at Malvolio*) Here he is, here he is. (*to Malvolio, amazed at the sight of his attire*) How are you, sir?

FABIAN
Here he is, here he is. How is't with you, sir?

SIR TOBY BELCH
How are you, man?

SIR TOBY BELCH
How is't with you, man?

MALVOLIO
Go away. I dismiss you. Leave me to my privacy. Go away.

MALVOLIO
Go off; I discard you. Let me enjoy my private. Go off.

MARIA
Listen how the devil speaks from deep within him! Didn't I tell you? – Sir Toby, my lady asks that you take care of him.

MARIA
Lo, how hollow the fiend speaks within him! Did not I tell you? Sir Toby, my lady prays you to have a care of him.

MALVOLIO
(*aside*) Ah ha! Does she now?

MALVOLIO
Ah ha! - does she so?

SIR TOBY BELCH (*to Maria*) Stop that, stop that. Hush, hush. We must deal with him gently. Leave it to me. (*to Malvolio*) How are you, Malvolio?	SIR TOBY BELCH Go to, go to. Peace, peace; we must deal gently with him. Let me alone. How do you, Malvolio?

SIR TOBY APPROACHES MALVOLIO CAUTIOUSLY.

SIR TOBY BELCH (CONT'D) How's everything with you? I say man, defy the devil. Remember he's an enemy to mankind.	SIR TOBY BELCH How is't with you? What, man, defy the devil. Consider, he's an enemy to mankind.
MALVOLIO (*pompously*) You are talking nonsense.	MALVOLIO Do you know what you say?
MARIA See! You speak ill of the devil and he takes it personally! Pray God he is not bewitched.	MARIA La you, and you speak ill of the devil, how he takes it at heart! Pray God he be not bewitched.
FABIAN Take a sample of his water to the wise woman.	FABIAN Carry his water* to th' wise woman.

**Note:* *'Water' – urine. To diagnose a patient the 'wise woman' would examine their urine. It was said the first passing of water of the day was the best to form a diagnosis with.*

MARIA Definitely, on my life it will be done first thing tomorrow morning. My lady would pay more money than I can count not to lose him.	MARIA Marry, and it shall be done tomorrow morning, if I live. My lady would not lose him for more than I'll say.
MALVOLIO What did you say, mistress?	MALVOLIO How now, mistress?

MARIA IS STARTLED BY MALVOLIO ADDRESSING HER AS 'MISTRESS'.

MARIA Oh, Lord!	MARIA O Lord!
SIR TOBY BELCH Please keep quiet. That's not the way, don't you see you upset him? Leave it to me.	SIR TOBY BELCH Prithee hold thy peace; this is not the way. Do you not see you move him? Let me alone with him.
FABIAN The only way is gentleness – gently, gently. The devil is rough, and won't allow a rough approach.	FABIAN No way but gentleness; gently, gently. The fiend is rough, and will not be roughly used.

SIR TOBY BELCH (*to Malvolio*) Why, how are you my old cock-sparrow? How are you, cocker?	SIR TOBY BELCH Why, how now, my bawcock? How dost thou, chuck?
MALVOLIO (*defiantly*) Sir!	MALVOLIO Sir!

SIR TOBY BECKONS TO MALVOLIO TO COME WITH HIM.

SIR TOBY BELCH Yes, chuck, come with me. What do you say, man? It's not dignified to play games with Satan. Hang him, foul devil.	SIR TOBY BELCH Ay, biddy, come with me. What, man, 'tis not for gravity to play at cherry-pit* with Satan. Hang him, foul collier!*

**Note: 'Cherry-pit' – children's game throwing cherry stones into a hole.*

'Collier' – Coal miner. The devil and coal miners both being black and underground.

MARIA Get him to say his prayers, good Sir Toby, get him to pray.	MARIA Get him to say his prayers, good Sir Toby, get him to pray.
MALVOLIO (*disdainful*) My prayers, minx?	MALVOLIO My prayers, minx?
MARIA (*shaking her head*) No, I'll bet he'll not want to hear of godliness.	MARIA No, I warrant you, he will not hear of godliness.
MALVOLIO Go hang yourselves, all of you! You ignorant, pathetic things. I'm not like you. As you'll discover soon enough.	MALVOLIO Go hang yourselves all! You are idle shallow things; I am not of your element. You shall know more hereafter.

EXIT MALVOLIO, STRUTTING WITH HIS NOSE IN THE AIR.

SIR TOBY BELCH Is it possible?	SIR TOBY BELCH Is't possible?
FABIAN If this was being acted out on a stage I would declare it an unbelievable work of fiction.	FABIAN If this were played upon a stage now, I could condemn it as an improbable fiction.
SIR TOBY BELCH He's fallen for our ploy completely, man.	SIR TOBY BELCH His very genius hath taken the infection of the device, man.
MARIA Pursue him, in case the effect of the ploy weakens.	MARIA Nay, pursue him now, lest the device take air and taint.

FABIAN We'll end up making him actually mad.	FABIAN Why, we shall make him mad indeed.
MARIA The house will be all the quieter for it.	MARIA The house will be the quieter.
SIR TOBY BELCH Come on, we'll shut him in a dark room and tie him up. My niece already believes he is mad, so we can carry this out for our pleasure and his pain till we tire of the game and have mercy on him, then we'll put our evidence before the court and crown Maria as champion judge of madmen.	SIR TOBY BELCH Come, we'll have him in a dark room and bound*. My niece is already in the belief that he's mad. We may carry it thus for our pleasure and his penance till our very pastime, tired out of breath, prompt us to have mercy on him; at which time we will bring the device to the bar, and crown thee for a finder* of madmen.

**Note: 'Dark room and bound" – Standard practice for mad people. Locked and tied up.*

'Finder' – Judge making a finding, or verdict.

ENTER SIR ANDREW CARRYING A PIECE OF PAPER.

SIR TOBY BELCH (CONT'D) (*seeing Sir Andrew*) But look who's here.	SIR TOBY BELCH But see, but see.
FABIAN More material for merriment.	FABIAN More matter for a May morning.*

**Note: 'May morning' – On 1st of May, all kinds of outrageous revelry was undertaken.*

SIR ANDREW AGUECHEEK (*waving letter*) Here's my challenge to him. Read it. I guarantee plenty of spice in it.	SIR ANDREW AGUECHEEK Here's the challenge; read it. I warrant there's vinegar and pepper in't.
FABIAN Is it saucy then?	FABIAN Is't so saucy?
SIR ANDREW AGUECHEEK (*missing the joke*) Aye, it is. I challenge him. Read it.	SIR ANDREW AGUECHEEK Ay, is't, I warrant him. Do but read.
SIR TOBY BELCH Give me it. (*reads*) "*Young man, whatever you are, you are nothing but a scurvy fellow.*"	SIR TOBY BELCH Give me. *[Reads.] "Youth, whatsoever thou art, thou art but a scurvy fellow."*
FABIAN Good, and strong.	FABIAN Good, and valiant.
SIR TOBY BELCH (*reads*) "*Don't wonder, or be surprised why I call you this, as I'll give you no reason for it.*"	SIR TOBY BELCH *[Reads.] "Wonder not, nor admire not in thy mind, why I do call thee so, for I will show thee no reason for't."*

FABIAN
A good letter, that keeps you within the bounds of the law.

FABIAN
A good note, that keeps you from the blow of the law.

SIR TOBY BELCH
(*reads*) *"You visit the Lady Olivia, and in front of me she treats you kindly, but you lie through your teeth. This is not the reason I am challenging you.*

SIR TOBY BELCH
[*Reads.*] *"Thou com'st to the Lady Olivia, and in my sight she uses thee kindly; but thou liest in thy throat; that is not the matter I challenge thee for."*

FABIAN
Brief and exceedingly good sense…
(*aside*) …less.

FABIAN
Very brief, and to exceeding good sense -
[*Aside.*] - less.*

**Note: 'Less' – i.e. 'senseless'.*

SIR TOBY BELCH
(*reads*) *"I will waylay you on your way home, whereby if you should chance to kill me…"*

SIR TOBY BELCH
[*Reads.*] *"I will waylay thee going home; where if it be thy chance to kill me," -*

FABIAN
Good.

FABIAN
Good.

SIR TOBY BELCH
(*reads*) *"…you will kill me like a rogue and a villain.*

SIR TOBY BELCH
[*Reads.*] *" - thou kill'st me like a rogue and a villain."*

FABIAN
Still you keep on the right side of the law, good.

FABIAN
Still you keep o'th' windy side of the law; good.

**Note: 'Windy side' – nautical term used in sailing. The advantageous side for progress.*

SIR TOBY BELCH
(*reads*) *"Farewell, and may God have mercy on one of our souls! He may have mercy on mine, but the outlook is better for me, so look out for yourself.*

Your friend, as you see fit, and your sworn enemy,

ANDREW AGUECHEEK."

If this letter doesn't move him, his legs don't work. I'll give it to him.

SIR TOBY BELCH
[*Reads.*] *"Fare thee well; and God have mercy upon one of our souls! He may have mercy upon mine, but my hope is better, and so look to thyself.*

Thy friend, as thou usest him, and thy sworn enemy,

ANDREW AGUECHEEK."

If this letter move him not, his legs cannot. I'll give't him.

MARIA
You have good occasion for it. He's here now talking some business with my lady, and will soon be leaving.

MARIA
You may have very fit occasion for't: he is now in some commerce with my lady, and will by-and-by depart.

SIR TOBY BELCH
Go, Sir Andrew, I'll send him to the corner of the garden. Wait in readiness with a surprise attack. As soon as you see him, draw your sword, and as you draw, swear terribly, as often a terrible oath, a sharp tongue and a swaggering manner, will give your manliness greater credibility than proving it with any action. Now go.

SIR TOBY BELCH
Go, Sir Andrew; scout me for him at the corner of the orchard like a bum-baily*. So soon as ever thou seest him, draw, and as thou draw'st, swear horrible; for it comes to pass oft that a terrible oath, with a swaggering accent sharply twanged off, gives manhood more approbation than ever proof itself would have earned him. Away.

**Note: 'Bum-baily' – a bailiff who sneaks up on debtors from behind.*

SIR TOBY PUSHES SIR ANDREW IN THE DIRECTION OF THE GARDEN.

SIR ANDREW AGUECHEEK
You can trust me on the swearing.

SIR ANDREW AGUECHEEK
Nay, let me alone for swearing.

EXIT SIR ANDREW WITHOUT HIS LETTER.

SIR TOBY BELCH
(*to Fabian, putting the letter in his pocket*) I won't deliver this letter, because the young gentleman's behaviour suggests good breeding, and intelligence. His use as a go-between for his lordship and my niece confirms this. Therefore this letter, being so exceedingly ignorant, will not incite any fear in the youth. He'll assume it comes from an idiot. Instead, sir, I shall deliver his challenge by word of mouth and make Aguecheek out as an extremely brave opponent, I'll scare the gentleman – who, being so young will believe it – with tales of his rage, skill, fury, and recklessness. They will both be so frightened that like a pair of basilisks they'll kill each other with just one look.

SIR TOBY BELCH
Now will not I deliver his letter, for the behaviour of the young gentleman gives him out to be of good capacity and breeding; his employment between his lord and my niece confirms no less. Therefore this letter, being so excellently ignorant, will breed no terror in the youth: he will find it comes from a clodpole. But, sir, I will deliver his challenge by word of mouth, set upon Aguecheek a notable report of valour, and drive the gentleman - as I know his youth will aptly receive it - into a most hideous opinion of his rage, skill, fury, and impetuosity. This will so fright them both that they will kill one another by the look, like cockatrices.*

**Note: 'Cockatrice' or Basilisk, a mythical creature which killed anyone by looking at them.*

It had the body of a dragon and the head of a cockerel.

RE-ENTER OLIVIA, WALKING WITH VIOLA (AS CESARIO).

FABIAN
Here he comes now with your niece. Let's stand aside till he leaves, then follow him.

FABIAN
Here he comes with your niece. Give them way till he take leave, and presently after him.

SIR TOBY BELCH I'll spend the time thinking up some fearful wording for a challenge.	SIR TOBY BELCH I will meditate the while upon some horrid message for a challenge.

SIR TOBY, FABIAN, AND MARIA QUIETLY LEAVE OLIVIA AND VIOLA ALONE.

OLIVIA I have said too much, laid my honour bare in a reckless manner, and my words fall upon a heart of stone. Something inside reprimands me for my wrongdoing, but it is such a headstrong stubborn wrongdoing that it defies reprimand.	OLIVIA I have said too much unto a heart of stone, And laid mine honour too unchary on't. There's something in me that reproves my fault; But such a headstrong potent fault it is That it but mocks reproof.
VIOLA (AS CESARIO) It is with the same passion that my master grieves.	VIOLA With the same haviour that your passion bears Goes on my master's griefs.

OLIVIA HANDS VIOLA (AS CESARIO) A LOCKET.

OLIVIA Here, wear this locket for me, it's my picture.	OLIVIA Here, wear this jewel for me, 'tis my picture.

VIOLA (AS CESARIO) MAKES NO ATTEMPT TO ACCEPT THE LOCKET.

OLIVIA (CONT'D) Don't refuse it, it won't bite you.	OLIVIA Refuse it not; it hath no tongue to vex you.

VIOLA RELUCTANTLY ALLOWS OLIVIA TO PLACE IT AROUND HIS/HER NECK.

OLIVIA (CONT'D) And I beg you, come again tomorrow. There is nothing you could ask from me that I would refuse - providing my honour is preserved.	OLIVIA And I beseech you come again tomorrow. What shall you ask of me that I'll deny, That honour saved may upon asking give?
VIOLA (AS CESARIO) Nothing but this – your true love for my master	VIOLA Nothing but this: your true love for my master
OLIVIA How can I keep my honour by giving him that? I've given it to you.	OLIVIA How with mine honour may I give him that Which I have given to you?
VIOLA (AS CESARIO) I will release you of any obligations to me..	VIOLA I will acquit you.

**Note:* *'Acquit' – release. Legal terms are littered throughout this play and many other Shakespeare plays. It would seem he had a keen interest in law and legal matters.*

OLIVIA
Well, come again tomorrow and farewell.
A fiend like you might take my soul to hell.

OLIVIA
Well, come again tomorrow. Fare thee well.
A fiend like thee might bear my soul to hell. *

**Note: 'A 'fiend' so charming and handsome may lead her to dishonourable behaviour, thereby damning her soul to hell.*

Note also the rhyming couplet as she leaves.

EXIT OLIVIA.

RE-ENTER SIR TOBY AND FABIAN WHO WERE WAITING FOR VIOLA TO BE ALONE

SIR TOBY BELCH
(*to Viola politely*) Gentleman, God save you.

SIR TOBY BELCH
Gentleman, God save thee.

VIOLA (AS CESARIO)
And you, sir.

VIOLA
And you, sir.

SIR TOBY BELCH
Whatever you have to defend yourself, ready it now. I don't know what wrongs you have done him, but your challenger is full of rage, and as hot-blooded as a hunter he awaits you at the end of the garden. Draw your rapier, make sure you are ready, your assailant is quick, skilful and deadly.

SIR TOBY BELCH
That defence thou hast, betake thee to't. Of what nature the wrongs are thou hast done him, I know not, but thy intercepter, full of despite, bloody as the hunter, attends thee at the orchard end. Dismount thy tuck*, be yare in thy preparation, for thy assailant is quick, skilful, and deadly.

**Note: 'Dismount thy tuck' – draw your rapier, a short, light sword for duelling and defence.*

VIOLA (AS CESARIO)
You must be mistaken, sir. I am certain no man has any quarrel with me. My memory is very clear about the lack of offence I've caused to any man.

VIOLA
You mistake, sir; I am sure no man hath any quarrel to me. My remembrance is very free and clear from any image of offence done to any man.

SIR TOBY BELCH
You'll find otherwise, I assure you. So, if you place any value on your life, be on guard. Your opponent has in him all the skills that youth, strength, skill and wrath can furnish a man with.

SIR TOBY BELCH
You'll find it otherwise, I assure you. Therefore, if you hold your life at any price, betake you to your guard; for your opposite hath in him what youth, strength, skill, and wrath can furnish man withal.

VIOLA (AS CESARIO)
(*worried*) I beg you tell me, sir, who is he?

VIOLA
I pray you, sir, what is he?

SIR TOBY BELCH
He was knighted with a ceremonial rapier, kneeling on a carpet rather than a battlefield, but he is a devil of a fighter. He has caused three souls to be separated from their bodies, and he's so incensed now that nothing short of death and burial will satisfy him. "Have, or have not" is his motto, take it or leave it.

SIR TOBY BELCH
He is knight dubbed with unhatched rapier and on carpet consideration, but he is a devil in private brawl. Souls and bodies hath he divorced three; and his incensement at this moment is so implacable that satisfaction can be none but by pangs of death and sepulchre. "Hob, nob"* is his word, give't or take't.

**Note: 'Hob, nob' – from old English dialect 'Habbe or Nabbe' meaning literally have or have not, or as he restates it, 'give or take'.*

VIOLA (AS CESARIO)
I will return to the house and request the lady provide me with an escort. I am not a fighter. I have heard about the kind of men who quarrel purposely with others to test their bravery, perhaps this a man of that ilk.

VIOLA
I will return again into the house and desire some conduct of the lady. I am no fighter. I have heard of some kind of men that put quarrels purposely on others to taste their valour: belike this is a man of that quirk.

VIOLA MAKES TO LEAVE BUT SIR TOBY PREVENTS HER/HIM.

SIR TOBY BELCH
No, sir. His anger stems from a very legally justifiable cause. So get on with it, and satisfy his desire. To go back to the house you'll have me to deal with, which is as much a danger as facing him. So get going, strip your sword stark naked, you must fight, that's for certain, or never wear a sword again.

SIR TOBY BELCH
Sir, no; his indignation derives itself out of a very competent injury; therefore get you on and give him his desire. Back you shall not to the house unless you undertake that with me which with as much safety you might answer him. Therefore on, or strip your sword stark naked; for meddle you must, that's certain, or forswear to wear iron about you.

VIOLA (AS CESARIO)
(*Aside*) This is as rude as it is bizarre.
(*to Sir Toby*) I beg of you this courtesy, let me know what my offence is to this knight. It must be my negligence to blame, not something I did on purpose.

VIOLA
This is as uncivil as strange. I beseech you do me this courteous office, as to know of the knight what my offence to him is. It is something of my negligence, nothing of my purpose.

SIR TOBY PAUSES, DELIBERATELY, TO FURTHER WORRY VIOLA.

SIR TOBY BELCH
…I will do that.
(*to Fabian*) Signor Fabian, wait with this gentleman till I return.

SIR TOBY BELCH
I will do so. Signor Fabian, stay you by this gentleman till my return.

EXIT SIR TOBY.

VIOLA (AS CESARIO) (*to Fabian*) If you please, sir, do you know anything about this matter?	VIOLA Pray you, sir, do you know of this matter?
FABIAN I know the knight is incensed with you, even to the point of mortal combat, but nothing about his reason.	FABIAN I know the knight is incensed against you, even to a mortal arbitrament, but nothing of the circumstance more.
VIOLA (AS CESARIO) I beg of you, what type of a man is he?	VIOLA I beseech you, what manner of man is he?
FABIAN To look at him, there is nothing in his appearance to suggest his bravery in action. But he is indeed, sir, the most skilful, bloody, deadly opponent that you could possibly meet in the whole of Illyria. Will you walk to him?	FABIAN Nothing of that wonderful promise, to read him by his form, as you are like to find him in the proof of his valour. He is indeed, sir, the most skilful, bloody, and fatal opposite that you could possibly have found in any part of Illyria. Will you walk towards him?

VIOLA (AS CESARIO) HESITATES, FEARFUL.

FABIAN (CONT'D) I will try to make peace with him on your behalf, if I can.	FABIAN I will make your peace with him if I can.
VIOLA (AS CESARIO) I would be greatly obliged to you if you did. I'd rather go with sir priest to the altar than sir knight to battle. I don't care who knows about my bravery.	VIOLA I shall be much bound to you for't. I am one that had rather go with sir priest* than sir knight. I care not who knows so much of my mettle.*

**Note: 'Sir priest' – Priests were addressed as 'sir' as well as knights of the realm.*

'Mettle' – a pun on bravery and using a metal sword.

EXEUNT FABIAN AND A VERY SCARED VIOLA.

RE-ENTER SIR TOBY WITH SIR ANDREW.

SIR TOBY BELCH (*to Sir Andrew*) Why, man, he's the very devil. I have never seen such a hellcat.	SIR TOBY BELCH Why, man, he's a very devil; I have not seen such a firago*.

**Note: 'Firago' – This is probably a deliberate mispronunciation and misunderstanding of the word 'virago' – which means an evil woman. He probably doesn't realise the irony of calling the youth by a female term.*

SIR ANDREW IS TAKEN ABACK. HIS FEAR GROWS AS SIR TOBY CONTINUES.

SIR TOBY BELCH (CONT'D)
I've had a bout with him, rapiers, all sheathed, and he delivers thrusts with such deadly accuracy they are unstoppable. And on the counter-thrust he finishes you off as surely as your feet are on the ground. They say he was the champion fencer of the Shah of Persia.

SIR TOBY BELCH
I had a pass with him, rapier, scabbard*, and all, and he gives me the stuck-in with such a mortal motion that it is inevitable; and on the answer he pays you as surely as your feet hits the ground they step on. They say he has been fencer to the Sophy.

**Note: "Scabbard' – the sheath the sword is held in, Toby throws in the line to explain why he survived the fencing by fighting with their sheathed swords.*

SIR ANDREW AGUECHEEK
A pox on it. I'll not quarrel with him.

SIR ANDREW AGUECHEEK
Pox on't, I'll not meddle with him.

SIR TOBY BELCH
Yes, but he will not be pacified. Fabian can scarce hold him back over there.

SIR TOBY BELCH
Ay, but he will not now be pacified. Fabian can scarce hold him yonder.

SIR TOBY INDICATES THE WAITING PAIR.

NOW IT IS SIR ANDREW'S TURN TO LOOK SCARED.

SIR ANDREW AGUECHEEK
A plague on it! If I'd known he was so brave and so skilful at fencing I'd have seen him damned rather than challenge him. If he will let the matter slide I'll give him my horse, Grey Capilet.

SIR ANDREW AGUECHEEK
Plague on't; and I thought he had been valiant and so cunning in fence I'd have seen him damned ere I'd have challenged him. Let him let the matter slip, and I'll give him my horse, grey Capilet.

ENTER FABIAN AND VIOLA. SIR TOBY SEES THEM APPROACHING.

SIR TOBY BELCH
(*to Sir Andrew*) I'll make the proposal. Stand here, make a show of bravado and this may end without loss of life.
(*aside as he walks away*) I'll take your horse for a merry ride as well as taking you for a ride.

SIR TOBY BELCH
I'll make the motion. Stand here, make a good show on't. This shall end without the perdition of souls.
[Aside.] Marry, I'll ride your horse as well as I ride you.

SIR TOBY APPROACHES FABIAN AND VIOLA, AND TAKES FABIAN ASIDE.

SIR TOBY BELCH (CONT'D)
(*aside to Fabian*) I've got his horse as a means to settle the argument. I've convinced him the youth is a devil.

SIR TOBY BELCH
[*Aside to Fabian.*] I have his horse to take up the quarrel. I have persuaded him the youth's a devil.

FABIAN (*aside to Sir Toby*) The youth is just as horribly in fear of him. He's breathing heavily and quite pale, as if a bear were chasing at his heels.	FABIAN [*Aside to Sir Toby.*] He is as horribly conceited of him, and pants and looks pale, as if a bear were at his heels.
SIR TOBY BELCH (*aloud to Viola)* There's no remedy, sir, he must fight with you for the sake of honour. Although, he has now thought better of his quarrel, and finds that it is now hardly worth talking of. So draw your sword in support of his honour, he promises he will not hurt you.	SIR TOBY BELCH [*To Viola.*] There's no remedy, sir; he will fight with you for's oath sake. Marry, he hath better bethought him of his quarrel, and he finds that now scarce to be worth talking of. Therefore draw for the supportance of his vow; he protests he will not hurt you.
VIOLA (AS CESARIO) (*aside*) Pray God defend me! The smallest thing would make me tell them how much I lack as a man.	VIOLA [*Aside.*] Pray God defend me! A little thing would make me tell them how much I lack of a man.
FABIAN (*aside to Sir Andrew*) Back off if you see him becoming angry.	FABIAN [*To Sir Andrew.*] Give ground if you see him furious.

SIR TOBY DRAWS THE COMBATANTS TOGETHER.

SIR TOBY BELCH (*aside to Sir Andrew)* Come, Sir Andrew, there's no other way. For the sake of honour the gentleman will have one bout with you, by the rules of duelling he cannot avoid it. But he has promised me, as a gentleman to a soldier, that he will not hurt you. (*aloud to both)* Come, take up your positions.	SIR TOBY BELCH Come, Sir Andrew, there's no remedy; the gentleman will for his honour's sake have one bout with you; he cannot by the duello avoid it; but he has promised me, as he is a gentleman and a soldier, he will not hurt you. Come on, to't.

SIR ANDREW DRAWS HIS SWORD, NERVOUSLY.

SIR ANDREW AGUECHEEK I pray to God he keeps his oath!	SIR ANDREW AGUECHEEK Pray God he keep his oath!

VIOLA (AS CESARIO) NERVOUSLY DRAWS HIS/HER SWORD.

VIOLA (AS CESARIO) I assure you I am against doing this.	VIOLA I do assure you 'tis against my will.

THE TWO SWING THEIR SWORDS INEFFECTIVELY, EYES HALF CLOSED, NOT IN DANGER OF MAKING ANY CONTACT.

ANTONIO (THE SEA CAPTAIN WHO RESCUED SEBASTIAN) ENTERS AND SEEING THE TWO WITH SWORDS DRAWN ASSUMES IT IS SEBASTIAN FIGHTING AND JUMPS IN TO PROTECT HIM.

Note: To show he is serious, Antonio speaks in blank verse, breaking the comedic prose.

ANTONIO (*to Sir Andrew*) Raise your sword. If this young gentleman has offended you, I'll answer for him. If you have offended him, on his behalf, I will face you.	ANTONIO Put up your sword. If this young gentleman Have done offence, I take the fault on me; If you offend him, I for him defy you.

ANTONIO DRAWS HIS SWORD.

SIR TOBY BELCH You, sir? Why, who are you?	SIR TOBY BELCH You, sir? - why, what are you?
ANTONIO A man, sir, who for the love of a comrade dares do more than you have heard him brag to you he'll do.	ANTONIO One, sir, that for his love dares yet do more Than you have heard him brag to you he will.
SIR TOBY BELCH No, if you fight for him, you fight me.	SIR TOBY BELCH Nay, if you be an undertaker*, I am for you.

**Note: 'Undertaker' – someone who undertakes the task on behalf of someone else.*

AS SIR TOBY DRAWS HIS SWORD, TWO OFFICERS OF THE LAW ARRIVE.

FABIAN Oh, good Sir Toby, wait - here come officers of the law.	FABIAN O good Sir Toby, hold: here come the officers.

SIR TOBY QUICKLY PUTS AWAY HIS SWORD.

SIR TOBY BELCH (*to Antonio*) I'll be with you shortly.	SIR TOBY BELCH [*To Antonio.*] I'll be with you anon.
VIOLA (AS CESARIO) (*to Sir Andrew, putting away her sword*) Please, sir, if you please, put away your sword.	VIOLA [*To Sir Andrew.*] Pray, sir, put your sword up, if you please.

SIR ANDREW PUTS AWAY HIS SWORD, VIOLA DOES LIKEWISE.

SIR ANDREW AGUECHEEK
(*relieved*) Indeed I will, sir, and as for my promise, I'll be as good as my word. He will carry you easily, and rides well.

SIR ANDREW AGUECHEEK
Marry, will I, sir; and for that I promised you I'll be as good as my word. He will bear you easily, and reins well.

SIR ANDREW AND VIOLA SHAKE HANDS, DISPUTE SETTLED, THOUGH VIOLA HAS NO IDEA THAT SIR ANDREW IS TALKING ABOUT DONATING HIS HORSE.

THE 1ST OFFICER INDICATES ANTONIO AND ORDERS THE 2ND OFFICER.

1ST OFFICER
This is the man, do your duty.

2ND OFFICER
Antonio, I arrest you on behalf of the lawsuit raised by the Count Orsino.

ANTONIO
You mistake me for another, sir.

1ST OFFICER
No, sir, not a bit. I know your face well, though now you have no sea-cap on your head. Take him away, he knows I know him well

ANTONIO
I will obey.

1ST OFFICER
This is the man; do thy office.

2ND OFFICER
Antonio, I arrest thee at the suit
Of Count Orsino.

ANTONIO
You do mistake me, sir.

1ST OFFICER
No, sir, no jot; I know your favour well,
Though now you have no sea-cap on your head.
Take him away; he knows I know him well.

ANTONIO
I must obey.

THE OFFICER APPREHENDS ANTONIO WHO CALLS OUT TO VIOLA BELIEVING SHE IS HER TWIN BROTHER SEBASTIAN.

ANTONIO
(*to Viola*) This is what comes from searching for you. But there's nothing that can be done, I'll answer the charge. How will you manage now that my necessity forces me to ask for my purse back? What I cannot do for you saddens me much more than what might befall you.

ANTONIO
[*To Viola.*] This comes with seeking you.
But there's no remedy; I shall answer it.
What will you do now my necessity
Makes me to ask you for my purse? It grieves me
Much more for what I cannot do for you
Than what befalls myself.

VIOLA IS CONFUSED.

ANTONIO (CONT'D)
You look bewildered, but don't worry about me.

2ND OFFICER
(*pulling Antonio away*) Come on, sir, let's go.

ANTONIO
(*to Viola*) I must beg for some of that money.

ANTONIO
You stand amazed,
But be of comfort.

2ND OFFICER
Come, sir, away.

ANTONIO
I must entreat of you some of that money.

VIOLA (AS CESARIO) What money, sir? For the great kindness you have shown me here, as well as in response of your current predicament, I can lend you something from my meagre means. I don't have much but I'll share what I have about my person with you.	VIOLA What money, sir? For the fair kindness you have showed me here, And part being prompted by your present trouble, Out of my lean and low ability I'll lend you something. My having is not much; I'll make division of my present with you.

VIOLA COUNTS OUT THE FEW COINS SHE HAS AND OFFERS HALF TO ANTONIO WHO KNOCKS THEM AWAY.

VIOLA (AS CESARIO) (CONT'D) Here, there's half of my money.	VIOLA Hold, there's half my coffer.
ANTONIO Do you refuse me now? Is it possible that all I've done for you is not persuasion enough? Don't provoke me in my misery to the point it makes me lose my respect and forces me to remind you of the past kindness I have shown you.	ANTONIO Will you deny me now? Is't possible that my deserts to you Can lack persuasion? Do not tempt my misery, Lest that it make me so unsound a man As to upbraid you with those kindnesses That I have done for you.
VIOLA (AS CESARIO) I don't know of any. Nor do I know you, by voice or by appearance. I hate ingratitude in a man more than lying, vanity, boasting, drunkenness, or any hint of a vice which strongly corrupts our weak bodies.	VIOLA I know of none, Nor know I you by voice or any feature. I hate ingratitude more in a man Than lying, vainness, babbling drunkenness, Or any taint of vice whose strong corruption Inhabits our frail blood.
ANTONIO (*disbelief*) Oh, by the heavens!	ANTONIO O heavens themselves!
2ND OFFICER Come, sir, you must leave.	2ND OFFICER Come, sir, I pray you go.
ANTONIO Let me speak a little. This youth that you see here, I snatched from the jaws of death, comforted him with such loving support, and devoted myself to his image as I believed him worthy of it.	ANTONIO Let me speak a little. This youth that you see here I snatched one half out of the jaws of death, Relieved him with such sanctity of love, And to his image, which methought did promise Most venerable worth, did I devotion.

**Note: Antonio is comparing his devotion to a religious one and is making out that he thought Sebastian was almost saintlike and worthy of such devotion.*

1ST OFFICER What's that got to do with us? We're wasting time, let's go.	1ST OFFICER What's that to us? The time goes by; away.
ANTONIO Oh, how vile an idol this god proves to be! Sebastian, you have shamed your face. *For nature's only fault is in the mind;* *The worst thing you can do is be unkind.* *Goodness is beauty, but the beauty of evil* *Is empty chests, overfilled by the devil.*	ANTONIO O how vile an idol proves this god! Thou hast, Sebastian, done good feature shame. *In nature there's no blemish but the mind;* *None can be called deformed but the unkind.* *Virtue is beauty, but the beauteous evil* *Are empty trunks, o'erflourished by the devil.*
1ST OFFICER The man is mad, take him away. Come along, sir.	1ST OFFICER The man grows mad; away with him. Come, come, sir.
ANTONIO Lead the way.	ANTONIO Lead me on.

THE OFFICERS LEAD ANTONIO AWAY.

VIOLA (AS CESARIO) *I think his words do with such passion say* *What he believes is true, for me, no way.* *Prove true my wildest thoughts, oh please prove true,* *That I, dear brother, was mistook for you.*	VIOLA *Methinks his words do from such passion fly* *That he believes himself; so do not I.* *Prove true, imagination, O prove true,* *That I, dear brother, be now ta'en for you!*
SIR TOBY BELCH Come here, knight, come here, Fabian. We'll exchange a line or two of wise words.	SIR TOBY BELCH Come hither, knight; come hither, Fabian. We'll whisper o'er a couplet or two of most sage saws.

THE THREE MEN STAND ASIDE.

VIOLA (AS CESARIO) *(aside) He said Sebastian. That is my brother.* *And in the mirror we look like each other.* *The way he dressed my brother did beguile,* *Clothed in this manner, same colour and style.*	VIOLA *He named Sebastian. I my brother know* *Yet living in my glass; even such and so* *In favour was my brother, and he went* *Still in this fashion, colour, ornament,*

VIOLA LOOKS DOWN AT HER MEN'S CLOTHING.

VIOLA (AS CESARIO) (CONT'D) *(aside) I imitate him, oh, let it be true,* *Tempests were kind, and salt waves loved him too.*	VIOLA *For him I imitate. O, if it prove,* *Tempests are kind, and salt waves fresh in love.*

VIOLA WALKS AWAY WITH A HAPPY SPRING IN HER STEP.

THE MEN WATCH HER LEAVE AND TALK ABOUT HER.

SIR TOBY BELCH
A very dishonourable, mean-spirited boy, more cowardly than a hare. His dishonesty shows in him leaving his friend here in need, and denying he knew him. And as for his cowardice – ask Fabian.

FABIAN
A coward, a most devout coward, he makes it his religion.

SIR ANDREW AGUECHEEK
Strewth, I'll go after him again and beat him.

SIR TOBY BELCH
A very dishonest paltry boy, and more a coward than a hare. His dishonesty appears in leaving his friend here in necessity, and denying him; and for his cowardship, ask Fabian.

FABIAN
A coward, a most devout coward, religious in it.

SIR ANDREW AGUECHEEK
'Slid, I'll after him again, and beat him.

**Note: ''Slid' – By God's eyelid. A mild oath.*

SIR TOBY BELCH
Do so. Don't draw your sword, but beat him soundly.

SIR ANDREW AGUECHEEK
(*now brave*) See if I don't!

SIR TOBY BELCH
Do; cuff him soundly, but never draw thy sword.

SIR ANDREW AGUECHEEK
An I do not –

EXIT SIR ANDREW AFTER VIOLA (AS CESARIO).

FABIAN
Come on, let's see this.

SIR TOBY BELCH
I'll wager any money that nothing will happen.

FABIAN
Come, let's see the event.

SIR TOBY BELCH
I dare lay any money 'twill be nothing yet.

EXEUNT.

ACT IV

ILLYRIA

OLIVIA'S HOUSE

"THAT THAT IS, IS."

ACT IV

ACT IV SCENE I

A STREET OUTSIDE OLIVIA'S HOUSE.

ENTER SEBASTIAN WITH FESTE FOLLOWING HIM.

FESTE Do you want me to believe that I was not sent to look for you?	FESTE Will you make me believe that I am not sent for you?
SEBASTIAN Go away, go away you foolish fellow. Let me be rid of you.	SEBASTIAN Go to, go to, thou art a foolish fellow. Let me be clear of thee.
FESTE You've kept up the act well, I swear. (*sarcastic*) No, I don't know you, nor have I been sent to find you by my lady to ask you to speak with her, nor is your name Master Cesario, nor is this (*he points*) my nose neither. Nothing is what it is.	FESTE Well held out, i'faith! No, I do not know you, nor I am not sent to you by my lady to bid you come speak with her, nor your name is not Master Cesario, nor this is not my nose neither. Nothing that is so is so.
SEBASTIAN Kindly vent your nonsense elsewhere. You don't know me.	SEBASTIAN I prithee vent thy folly somewhere else; Thou know'st not me.
FESTE (*mocking*) Vent my nonsense! (*aside to audience*) He has heard that word spoken by a great man, and now applies it to a fool. Vent my nonsense! I'm afraid this dumb world is becoming even dumber. (*to Sebastian*) I ask you, stop pretending you do not know me and tell me what I shall 'vent' to my lady. Shall I 'vent' to her that you are coming?	FESTE Vent my folly! He has heard that word of some great man, and now applies it to a fool. Vent my folly! I am afraid this great lubber, the world, will prove a cockney*. I prithee now, ungird thy strangeness and tell me what I shall vent to my lady. Shall I vent to her that thou art coming?

**Note: 'Cockney' – conceited. Now means a Londoner, which came from the meaning 'not country wise' or a townsperson who was overly mothered or spoilt.*

SEBASTIAN
I beg you, foolish jester, leave me. Here's money for you. If you stay any longer I shall pay you with something worse.

SEBASTIAN
I prithee, foolish Greek, depart from me.
There's money for thee. If you tarry longer
I shall give worse payment.*

**Note: 'Greek' – a merry Greek was a term for a cheerful joker, probably a corruption of the word 'grig' which is a cricket, and the term 'merry as a cricket'.*

'Worse payment' – a threat of violence.

SEBASTIAN OFFERS FESTE A COIN.

FESTE
Upon my word, you have a generous hand. (*aside*) These wise men who give fools money to get a good reputation – it will take fourteen years to purchase.

FESTE
By my troth, thou hast an open hand. These wise men that give fools money get themselves a good report - after fourteen years' purchase.*

**Note: 'Fourteen years' purchase' – to calculate the price of a house was to multiply a year's rent times twelve. Feste is saying it will take fourteen years to purchase a good reputation from him, not twelve.*

ENTER SIR ANDREW, SIR TOBY AND FABIAN.

SIR ANDREW SEES SEBASTIAN AND ASSUMES IT IS VIOLA.

SIR ANDREW AGUECHEEK
Now sir, have I met you again? This is for you!

SIR ANDREW AGUECHEEK
Now sir, have I met you again? There's for you!

SIR ANDREW STRIKES SEBASTIAN.

SEBASTIAN
Well, this is for you! And this, and this!

SEBASTIAN
Why, there's for thee - and there, and there!

SEBASTIAN BEATS SIR ANDREW WITH THE HANDLE OF HIS DAGGER.

SEBASTIAN (CONT'D)
Is everyone here mad?

SEBASTIAN
Are all the people mad?

SIR TOBY RESTRAINS AND HOLDS SEBASTIAN.

SIR TOBY BELCH
Stop, sir, or I'll throw your dagger over the wall.

SIR TOBY BELCH
Hold, sir, or I'll throw your dagger o'er the house.

FESTE This I have to tell my lady immediately. I wouldn't like to be in your shoes for twopence.	FESTE This will I tell my lady straight. I would not be in some of your coats for twopence.

EXIT FESTE TO TELL THE STORY TO LADY OLIVIA.

SIR TOBY BELCH (*to Sebastian*) Come with us, sir.	SIR TOBY BELCH Come on, sir,

SEBASTIAN STRUGGLES.

SIR TOBY BELCH (CONT'D) Stay.	SIR TOBY BELCH hold.
SIR ANDREW AGUECHEEK No, let him be.	SIR ANDREW AGUECHEEK Nay, let him alone;

SIR ANDREW RUBS HIS ACHING HEAD.

SIR ANDREW AGUECHEEK (CONT'D) I have another way to get even with him. I'll take out a lawsuit of battery against him, (*sarcastic*) if there is any law left in Illyria. Though I did strike him first, but no matter.	SIR ANDREW AGUECHEEK I'll go another way to work with him. I'll have an action of battery against him, if there be any law in Illyria. Though I stroke him first, yet it's no matter for that.
SEBASTIAN Let go of me!	SEBASTIAN Let go thy hand.
SIR TOBY BELCH Come along, sir, I will not let go of you. Come along, my young soldier, put away your dagger, you are already bloodied. Come along.	SIR TOBY BELCH Come, sir, I will not let you go. Come, my young soldier, put up your iron; you are well fleshed. Come on.
SEBASTIAN I will be free of you.	SEBASTIAN I will be free from thee.

SEBASTIAN FREES HIMSELF AND CONFRONTS SIR TOBY.

SEBASTIAN (CONT'D) What will you do now?	SEBASTIAN What wouldst thou now?

SEBASTIAN DRAWS HIS SWORD.

SEBASTIAN (CONT'D) If you dare to test me further, draw you sword.	SEBASTIAN If thou dar'st tempt me further, draw thy sword.
SIR TOBY BELCH What, what?	SIR TOBY BELCH What, what?

SIR TOBY DRAWS HIS SWORD DRUNKENLY.

SIR TOBY BELCH (CONT'D) Yes, and then I'll take an ounce or two of this impudent blood from you.	SIR TOBY BELCH Nay, then I must have an ounce or two of this malapert blood from you.

ENTER OLIVIA WHO STRIDES IN-BETWEEN THE TWO FIGHTERS.

OLIVIA Stop, Toby! Upon your life I order you to stop!	OLIVIA Hold, Toby! On thy life I charge thee hold.
SIR TOBY BELCH Madam.	SIR TOBY BELCH Madam.

SIR TOBY LOWERS HIS SWORD.

OLIVIA (*to Sir Toby*) Will it always be like this? Ungrateful wretch, fit only for the mountains and the barbarous caves where manners are never taught. Get out of my sight! (*to Sebastian*) Don't be offended, dear Cesario. (*to Sir Toby who still stands there*) Ill-mannered oaf, be gone!	OLIVIA Will it be ever thus? Ungracious wretch, Fit for the mountains and the barbarous caves, Where manners ne'er were preached. Out of my sight! Be not offended, dear Cesario. Rudesby, be gone!

EXIT SIR TOBY, SIR ANDREW, AND FABIAN WITH THEIR TAILS BETWEEN THEIR LEGS.

OLIVIA (CONT'D) I beg you, gentle friend, let your common-sense, rather than your anger, hold sway in this disgraceful and unlawful assault upon yourself. Come with me to my house, If I tell you how many pointless pranks that ruffian has thrown together, then you may find yourself smiling at this one. I insist you go. *Do not say no, but curse his soul for me,* *He startled my poor heart, which beats for thee.*	OLIVIA I prithee, gentle friend, Let thy fair wisdom, not thy passion, sway In this uncivil and unjust extent Against thy peace. Go with me to my house, And hear thou there how many fruitless pranks This ruffian hath botched up, that thou thereby Mayst smile at this. Thou shalt not choose but go; *Do not deny. Beshrew his soul for me;* *He started one poor heart of mine in thee.*

OLIVIA STARTS WALKING AWAY EXPECTING SEBASTIAN TO FOLLOW.

SEBASTIAN STANDS IN BEWILDERMENT, NOT UNDERSTANDING WHAT SHE IS TALKING ABOUT NOR WHY HE WAS SUDDENLY ATTACKED.

SEBASTIAN
(aside)
What sense is there in this? What does it mean?
Or am I mad and is this all a dream?
So, calm my thoughts before they run too deep.
If this is all a dream, then let me sleep;

SEBASTIAN
(aside)
What relish is in this? How runs the stream?
Or I am mad or else this is a dream.
Let fancy still my sense in Lethe steep;*
If it be thus to dream, still let me sleep.

**Note: 'Lethe' – the river of forgetfulness. A river in Hades, the land of the dead, whose water when drunk made souls forget their life on earth.*

OLIVIA STOPS AND SEES SEBASTIAN IS NOT FOLLOWING.

OLIVIA
Now, come with me, I wish you would obey!

OLIVIA
Nay, come, I prithee. Would thou'dst be ruled by me!

SEBASTIAN
(*still confused*)
I will, madam.

SEBASTIAN
Madam, I will.

OLIVIA
Oh, be those words you say.

OLIVIA
O, say so, and so be.

EXEUNT.

ACT IV SCENE II

A ROOM IN OLIVIA'S HOUSE.

ENTER FESTE AND MARIA CARRYING A RELIGIOUS GOWN AND A FALSE BEARD.

MARIA
Now, put on this gown and this beard. Make him believe you are Sir Topas the priest. Quickly now. I'll call Sir Toby while you do.

MARIA
Nay, I prithee put on this gown and this beard. Make him believe thou art Sir Topas* the curate; do it quickly. I'll call Sir Toby the whilst.

**Note: 'Sir Topas' – though Sir Topas was a name often used for a comical knight dating back to Chaucer's Rime of Sir Thopas. Here Shakespeare uses the name for a priest (hence the 'Sir') and possibly also chosen for the belief that the precious stone topaz possessed the power to cure mental illness.*

EXIT MARIA.

FESTE
(*aside*) Well, I'll put it on, and play the part. I'd like to think I was the first hypocrite ever to hide behind such a gown. I'm not fat enough to be a convincing priest, nor thin enough to be thought of as a good student, but to be seen as an honourable man and a generous host is as good as being a frugal man and a good scholar.

FESTE
Well, I'll put it on, and I will dissemble myself in't; and I would I were the first that ever dissembled in such a gown. I am not tall* enough to become the function well, nor lean enough to be thought a good student; but to be said an honest man and a good housekeeper goes as fairly as to say a careful man and a great scholar.

**Note: 'Tall' – Robert Armin, the actor who originally played the part, was an extremely short man, so this would have been amusing to the audience, especially if he donned a normal sized cloak. Without a short actor the word 'fat' makes more sense than 'tall'.*

RE-ENTER MARIA WITH SIR TOBY. FESTE PRETENDS TO BE A CLERGYMAN.

FESTE (CONT'D)
The partners in crime enter.

SIR TOBY BELCH
God bless you, Master Parson.

FESTE
Bonos dies, Sir Toby.

FESTE
The competitors enter.

SIR TOBY BELCH
Jove bless thee, Master Parson.

FESTE
Bonos dies, Sir Toby;

**Note: 'Bonos dies' – he pretends to speak in Latin, as a member of the clergy would, but mispronounces the words. He should say 'bonus' dies – good day.*

FESTE (CONT'D) And as the old hermit of Prague who could neither read nor write very wittily said to the niece of King Gorboduc, "That that is, is". So I, being Master Parson, *am* Master Parson, for what is the meaning of 'that' if not that, and 'is' if not is?	FESTE for as the old hermit of Prague that never saw pen and ink very wittily said to a niece of King Gorboduc*, "That that is, is"; so I being Master Parson, am Master Parson; for what is `that' but that, and `is' but is?

**Note: 'King Gorboduc' – A legendary king of England whose niece, as legend has it, knitted a pair of socks for the hermit of Prague*

SIR TOBY INDICATES A CLOSED DOOR.

SIR TOBY BELCH Go speak to him, Sir Topas.	SIR TOBY BELCH To him, Sir Topas.

FESTE CALLS THROUGH A HIGH GRILL IN A DOOR INTO ANOTHER ROOM WHERE MALVOLIO IS BEING KEPT PRISONER IN DARKNESS.

MALVOLIO CANNOT SEE ANYTHING OUTSIDE OF THE ROOM HE IS LOCKED IN.

FESTE (*calling to Malvolio*) How are you, I say. May peace be in this prison!	FESTE What ho, I say; peace in this prison!*

**Note: 'Peace...' - from the Book of Common Prayer (1559), "The Priest entering into the sick person's house, shall say 'Peace be in this house'."*

SIR TOBY BELCH (*to Maria*) The rogue impersonates well – a good rogue.	SIR TOBY BELCH The knave counterfeits well - a good knave.

MALVOLIO REPLIES WOEFULLY FROM THE ROOM IN WHICH HE IS HELD PRISONER

MALVOLIO (*off*) Who's there?	MALVOLIO [*within*] Who calls there?
FESTE Sir Topas the priest, he comes to visit Malvolio the lunatic.	FESTE Sir Topas the curate, who comes to visit Malvolio the lunatic.
MALVOLIO (*off*) Sir Topas, Sir Topas, good Sir Topas, go fetch my lady.	MALVOLIO [*within*] Sir Topas, Sir Topas, good Sir Topas, go to my lady.

FESTE NOW PRETENDS TO BE EXORCISING A DEVIL WHICH HAS SUPPOSEDLY POSSESSED MALVOLIO.

FESTE
Out, hyperbolical fiend! Why do you torment this man! Do you talk of nothing but ladies?

FESTE
Out, hyperbolical* fiend! How vexest thou this man! Talkest thou nothing but of ladies?

**Note: 'Hyperbolical' – Feste means diabolical but in trying to sound learned he confuses words. Hyperbolical means greatly exaggerated statements.*

FESTE SHAKES HIS HEAD AND TUTS DISAPPROVINGLY.

SIR TOBY BELCH
Well said, Master Parson.

SIR TOBY BELCH
Well said, Master Parson.

MALVOLIO
(*off*) Sir Topas, never was a man more wronged. Good Sir Topas, please don't think I'm mad. They have laid me here in hideous darkness.

MALVOLIO
[*within*] Sir Topas, never was man thus wronged. Good Sir Topas, do not think I am mad. They have laid me here in hideous darkness.

**Note: 'Laid me here' – suggesting being laid out in a mausoleum or tomb.*

FESTE
I defy you, dishonest Satan! I call you by the most moderate terms, because I am one of those polite souls who will treat even the devil himself with common courtesy. You say the house is dark?

FESTE
Fie, thou dishonest Satan! I call thee by the most modest terms, for I am one of those gentle ones that will use the devil himself with courtesy. Sayst thou that house is dark?

MALVOLIO
(*off*) As hell, Sir Topas.

MALVOLIO
[*within*] As hell, Sir Topas.

FESTE
Why, the bay windows of the house form transparent barricades, and the high windows from the north to the south are as bright as ebony, yet you complain of obstruction?

FESTE
Why, it hath bay windows transparent as barricadoes, and the clerestories toward the south-north are as lustrous as ebony; and yet complainest thou of obstruction?

MALVOLIO
(*off*) I am not mad, Sir Topas. I am telling you this house is dark.

MALVOLIO
[*within*] I am not mad, Sir Topas. I say to you this house is dark.

FESTE
Madman, you are wrong. I say the only darkness is ignorance, in which you are more enveloped than the Egyptians when the Lord plunged their land into darkness.

FESTE
Madman, thou errest. I say there is no darkness but ignorance, in which thou art more puzzled than the Egyptians in their fog.*

**Note: 'Fog' – the ninth plague sent by God upon the Egyptians for refusing to let the Israelites leave. Thick darkness 'which could be felt' enveloped the country of Egypt.*

MALVOLIO
(*off*) I tell you this house is as dark as ignorance, ignorance as dark as hell. And I say there was never a man more abused than me. I am no more mad than you are. Test me with any relevant question.

FESTE
What is the opinion of Pythagorus concerning wildfowl?

MALVOLIO
[*within*] I say this house is as dark as ignorance, though ignorance were as dark as hell; and I say there was never man thus abused. I am no more mad than you are; make the trial of it in any constant question.

FESTE
What is the opinion of Pythagoras* concerning wildfowl?

**Note: 'Pythagoras' - Greek philosopher - famous to schoolchildren for his rules of trigonometry – but also a believer that souls could migrate between animals and humans.*

MALVOLIO
(*off*) That the soul of our grandmother might perhaps inhabit a bird.

FESTE
What do you think of his opinion?

MALVOLIO
(*off*) I think the soul is noble and in no way approve of his opinion.

FESTE
Farewell. Remain in the darkness. You must agree to the opinion of Pythagoras before I will certify you as sane. That is, when you're afraid to kill a dumb woodcock for fear that you displace the soul of your grandmother. Farewell.

MALVOLIO
[*within*] That the soul of our grandam might haply inhabit a bird.

FESTE
What think'st thou of his opinion?

MALVOLIO
[*within*] I think nobly of the soul, and no way approve his opinion.

FESTE
Fare thee well; remain thou still in darkness. Thou shalt hold th' opinion of Pythagoras ere I will allow of thy wits, and fear to kill a woodcock* lest thou dispossess the soul of thy grandam. Fare thee well.

**Note: 'Woodcock' – a proverbially stupid bird. Suggesting his grandmother (and therefore his lineage) was stupid.*

MALVOLIO
(*off*) Sir Topas! Sir Topas!

SIR TOBY BELCH
Exquisitely done, Sir Topas!

FESTE
(*to Sir Toby*) I am very versatile.

MARIA
You could have done this without the beard and gown as he can't see you.

MALVOLIO
[*within*] Sir Topas, Sir Topas.

SIR TOBY BELCH
My most exquisite Sir Topas.

FESTE
Nay, I am for all waters.

MARIA
Thou mightst have done this without thy beard and gown - he sees thee not.

SIR TOBY BELCH
(*to Feste*) Talk to him using your own voice, and let me know how he is.
(*to Maria*) I'd rather we were well rid of this fooling. If he can be released without any fuss, I'd rather he was, as I am now in so much trouble with my niece that I can no longer safely pursue this hoax to the end.
(*to Feste*) Come to my room shortly.

SIR TOBY BELCH
To him in thine own voice, and bring me word how thou find'st him.
[*To Maria.*] I would we were well rid of this knavery. If he may be conveniently delivered, I would he were; for I am now so far in offence with my niece that I cannot pursue with any safety this sport to the upshot.
[*To Feste.*] Come by-and-by to my chamber.

EXEUNT SIR TOBY AND MARIA. FESTE STOPS BEING SIR TOPAS.

FESTE
(sings) "Hey Robin, jolly Robin,
Tell me how my lady is."

FESTE
[Sings.] "Hey Robin, jolly Robin,
*Tell me how thy lady does."**

**Note: 'Hey Robin...' – Feste sings an old ballad which says that women can only be trusted to be untrustworthy.*

MALVOLIO
(*off*) Fool?

MALVOLIO
[*within*] Fool?

FESTE
(sings) "My lady is unkind, by God."

FESTE
*[Sings.] "My lady is unkind, perdie."**

**Note: 'Perdie' – by God. From the French 'par dieu'.*

MALVOLIO
(*off louder*) Fool?

MALVOLIO
[*within*] Fool?

FESTE
(sings) "Alas, why is she so?"

FESTE
[Sings.] "Alas, why is she so?"

MALVOLIO
(*off very loud*) Fool, I say!

MALVOLIO
[*within*] Fool, I say.

FESTE
(sings) "She loves another..."
Who calls, eh?

FESTE
[Sings.] "She loves another -"
Who calls, ha?

MALVOLIO
(*off*) Good fool, if you want to be always held in my good esteem, help me to a candle, a pen and some paper. On my honour as a gentleman, I will be forever grateful to you for it.

MALVOLIO
[*within*] Good fool, as ever thou wilt deserve well at my hand, help me to a candle, and pen, ink, and paper. As I am a gentleman, I will live to be thankful to thee for't.

FESTE
Master Malvolio?

FESTE
Master Malvolio?

MALVOLIO
(*off*) Yes, good fool.

MALVOLIO
[*within*] Ay, good fool.

FESTE
Alas, sir, how did you come to lose your wits?

FESTE
Alas, sir, how fell you besides your five wits?

MALVOLIO
(*off*) Fool, never was a man so shamefully abused. I have as many of my wits about me as you do.

MALVOLIO
[*within*] Fool, there was never man so notoriously abused; I am as well in my wits, fool, as thou art.

FESTE
As many? Then you are indeed mad if you have no more wits than a fool.

FESTE
But as well? Then you are mad indeed if you be no better in your wits than a fool.

MALVOLIO
(*off*) They have abused me, kept me in darkness, and sent priests to me – the asses! – to try to drive me out of my wits.

MALVOLIO
[*within*] They have here propertied me, keep me in darkness, send ministers to me - asses! -and do all they can to face me out of my wits.

FESTE
Careful what you say, the priest is here.
(*as Sir Topas*) Malvolio, Malvolio, may heaven restore your wits! Try to get some sleep, and stop your vain babbling.

FESTE
Advise you what you say: the minister is here.
[*As Sir Topas.*] Malvolio, Malvolio, thy wits the heavens restore! Endeavour thyself to sleep, and leave thy vain bibble-babble.

MALVOLIO
(*off*) Sir Topas!

MALVOLIO
[*within*] Sir Topas!

FESTE
(*as Sir Topas to himself as Feste)* Don't talk to him, good fellow.
(*replying as himself)* Who, me, sir? Not I, sir. God be with you, good Sir Tobas.
(*as Sir Topas*) Indeed, amen!

FESTE
[*As Sir Topas.*] Maintain no words with him, good fellow.
[*As himself.*] Who, I, sir? Not I, sir. God-buy-you, good Sir Topas.
[*As Sir Topas.*] Marry, amen!

FESTE PRETENDS THE IMAGINARY PRIEST IS LEAVING AND HE CALLS AFTER HIM.

FESTE (CONT'D)
(*as himself*) I will, sir, I will.

FESTE
[*As himself.*] I will, sir, I will.

MALVOLIO
(*off*) Fool, fool, fool, I say!

MALVOLIO
[*within*] Fool, fool, fool, I say!

FESTE
Alas, sir, be patient. What do you want, sir? I'll be in trouble for talking to you.

FESTE
Alas, sir, be patient. What say you, sir? I am shent* for speaking to you.

**Note: 'Shent' – rebuked, by the imaginary priest who said not to talk with Malvolio.*

MALVOLIO
(*off*) Good fool, help me get some light and paper. I tell you, I am as sane as any man in Illyria.

MALVOLIO
[*within*] Good fool, help me to some light and some paper. I tell thee I am as well in my wits as any man in Illyria.

FESTE Alas, I wish you were, sir!	FESTE Welladay* that you were, sir!

Note: 'Welladay' – alas, from Wellaway, which is from Anglo Saxon, Woe! Lo! Woe

MALVOLIO (*off*) I swear I am. Good fool, some ink, paper, and a light, and carry what I will write down to my lady. It will be much more profitable to you than carrying any other letter.	MALVOLIO [*within*] By this hand, I am. Good fool, some ink, paper, and light; and convey what I will set down to my lady. It shall advantage thee more than ever the bearing of letter did.
FESTE I will help you with it. But tell me the truth, are you really mad or are you pretending?	FESTE I will help you to't. But tell me true, are you not mad indeed, or do you but counterfeit?
MALVOLIO (*off*) Believe me, I am not mad. I'm telling the truth!	MALVOLIO [*within*] Believe me, I am not; I tell thee true.
FESTE Ha, I'll never believe a madman till I see he is dead. I will fetch you light, paper and ink.	FESTE Nay, I'll ne'er believe a madman till I see his brains. I will fetch you light and paper and ink.
MALVOLIO (*off*) Fool, I'll reward you in the highest degree. I beg you, be gone.	MALVOLIO [*within*] Fool, I'll requite it in the highest degree. I prithee be gone.
FESTE *(sings) "I am gone, sir,* *And anon, sir,* *I'll be with you again,* *In a trice,* *Like to the old Vice,* *Your need to sustain;* *Who with dagger of wood,* *In a rage and foul mood,* *Cries 'Ah, ha!' to the devil.* *Like a mad lad,* *'Trim your nails, dad.'* *Adieu, goodman devil"*	FESTE *[Sings.] "I am gone, sir,* *And anon, sir,* *I'll be with you again,* *In a trice,* *Like to the old Vice,* * *Your need to sustain;* *Who with dagger of lath,* * *In his rage and his wrath,* *Cries `Ah, ha!' to the devil.* *Like a mad lad,* *`Pare thy nails, dad.'* *Adieu, goodman devil"*

Note: 'Vice' - A character in morality plays which were old even in Shakespeare's time. A mischievous character in league with the devil, using farce and slapstick against other characters, mainly the virtuous hero.

'Lath' – wood. The Vice carried a wooden dagger with which he would jump on the devil's back and beat him about the head and threaten to trim his long nails.

There is no known source for this song.

ACT IV SCENE III

OLIVIA'S GARDEN.

ENTER SEBASTIAN, TRYING TO MAKE SENSE OF EVERYTHING.

SEBASTIAN

(*sniffing*) This is the air,
(*looks up to the sky*) there is the glorious sun, (*he holds a pearl up to the sky*) and this is the pearl she gave me. I can feel it and see it, so though I am wrapped in wonder, it's not madness at least. Where's Antonio got to? He wasn't at the Elephant Inn. I was told he'd been there and was now searching the town for me. His advice would be invaluable right now, for though my mind is at odds with my senses, I may be mistaken rather than mad. But these unexpected good fortunes are so far in excess that I'm doubting my own eyes, and the only conclusion I can come to is that either I am mad or the lady is. But if she is mad, she could not run her house, manage her staff, administer her affairs and sign them off with such efficiency and noble bearing as I perceive she does. There's something not right in all this.
But here comes the lady now.

SEBASTIAN

This is the air, that is the glorious sun;
This pearl she gave me, I do feel't and see't,
And though 'tis wonder that enwraps me thus,
Yet 'tis not madness. Where's Antonio then?
I could not find him at the Elephant;
Yet there he was, and there I found this credit,
That he did range the town to seek me out.
His counsel now might do me golden service,
For though my soul disputes well with my sense
That this may be some error, but no madness,
Yet doth this accident and flood of fortune
So far exceed all instance, all discourse,
That I am ready to distrust mine eyes,
And wrangle with my reason that persuades me
To any other trust but that I am mad
Or else the lady's mad. Yet if 'twere so,
She could not sway her house, command her followers,
Take and give back affairs and their dispatch,
With such a smooth, discreet, and stable bearing
As I perceive she does. There's something in't
That is deceivable. But here the lady comes.

ENTER OLIVIA WITH A PRIEST.

OLIVIA

(*to Sebastian*) Forgive my haste, but if your intentions are honourable, come with this holy man and I to the chapel nearby. Before him, underneath the consecrated roof, pledge yourself to me, so that my most jealous and doubtful heart may live in peace. He will not make it public until we have arranged a wedding ceremony suitable for one of my social standing. What do you say?

OLIVIA

Blame not this haste of mine. If you mean well,
Now go with me and with this holy man
Into the chantry by. There, before him
And underneath that consecrated roof,
Plight me the full assurance of your faith,
That my most jealous and too doubtful soul
May live at peace. He shall conceal it
Whiles you are willing it shall come to note,
What time we will our celebration keep
According to my birth. What do you say?

SEBASTIAN
I'll follow this good man, and go with you;
To swear my heart forever will be true.

OLIVIA
Then lead the way, father, and may heavens shine
Their blessings down on this holy act of mine!

SEBASTIAN
I'll follow this good man, and go with you;
And having sworn truth, ever will be true.

OLIVIA
Then lead the way, good father, and heavens so shine
That they may fairly note this act of mine!

ACT V

ILLYRIA

OLIVIA'S HOUSE

"ONE FACE, ONE VOICE, ONE HABIT, AND TWO PERSONS"

ACT V

ACT V SCENE I

A STREET OUTSIDE OLIVIA'S HOUSE.

ENTER FESTE CARRYING A LETTER, ACCOMPANIED BY FABIAN.

FABIAN
Come on, as my friend, let me see his letter.

FESTE
Good Master Fabian, only if you grant my request.

FABIAN
Anything.

FESTE
Do not ask to see this letter.

FABIAN
That's like giving away my dog, and in return asking for it back again.

FABIAN
Now as thou lov'st me, let me see his letter.

FESTE
Good Master Fabian, grant me another request.

FABIAN
Anything.

FESTE
Do not desire to see this letter.

FABIAN
This is to give a dog, and in recompense desire my dog again.*

**Note: From an event recorded in the diary of John Manningham – Dr Boleyn, Queen Elizabeth's kinsman, had a dog which he doted on. Noticing this, the queen requested that he grant her one desire, and in return she would grant him whatsoever he asked for. He had to agree, it was dangerous to disagree with the monarch. She demanded his dog. He gave it to her saying, 'Madam, you promised in return to give me whatsoever I desired". "I will," she replied. "Then, madam, I ask that you give me my dog back again".*

ENTER DUKE ORSINI, VIOLA (AS CESARIO), CURIO AND LORDS.

DUKE ORSINI
Are you members of Lady Olivia's household, my friends?

FESTE
Yes, sir, we are some of her adornments.

DUKE ORSINI
Belong you to the Lady Olivia, friends?

FESTE
Ay, sir, we are some of her trappings.

**Note: 'Trappings' – adornments which go with a role, derived from a horse's ornamental harness.*

DUKE ORSINI
I know you well! How are you, my good fellow?

DUKE ORSINI
I know thee well. How dost thou, my good fellow?

FESTE
Truly, sir, all the better for having enemies, and all the worse for having friends.

FESTE
Truly, sir, the better for my foes and the worse for my friends.

DUKE ORSINI
On the contrary, it's all the better for having friends.

DUKE ORSINI
Just the contrary: the better for thy friends.

FESTE
No, sir, it's worse.

FESTE
No, sir, the worse.

DUKE ORSINI
How is that?

DUKE ORSINI
How can that be?

FESTE
Because, sir, they praise me, which makes an ass of me. Now, my foes tell me bluntly that I am an ass, so from my foes, sir, I learn more about myself, but by my friends I am deceived. So, if conclusions were kisses, if your four negatives make your two positives, if works out worse for my friends and better for my enemies.

FESTE
Marry, sir, they praise me and make an ass of me. Now my foes tell me plainly I am an ass; so that by my foes, sir, I profit in the knowledge of myself, and by my friends I am abused; so that, conclusions to be as kisses, if your four negatives make your two affirmatives, why, then the worse for my friends, and the better for my foes.*

**Note: The logic here is based on the grammatic rule that two negatives make a positive.*

A common joke based on this logic was that when a maid was asked for a kiss, if she replied, 'No, no' she really meant yes. Some scholars suggest that the four negatives are the lips of two lovers (two each) who quarrel and then make up by kissing, producing a positive of two sets of lips. (two double negatives make two positives).

Feste admits himself that he is a corrupter of words, in which case many conclusions may be drawn from his statement above. But at the core it all boils down to; four negative statements from your enemies equals two positive statements, and four positive statements from your friends equals two negatives.

DUKE ORSINI
Why, this is excellent.

DUKE ORSINI
Why, this is excellent.

FESTE
Upon my word, sir, it is not. Though if it pleases you, you can be one of my friends.

FESTE
By my troth, sir, no; though it please you to be one of my friends.

FESTE HOLD OUT HIS HAND FOR A TIP.

DUKE ORSINI You shall not be worse off by me flattering you. Here's gold instead.	DUKE ORSINI Thou shalt not be the worse for me. There's gold.

ORSINI HANDS FESTE A GOLD COIN.

FESTE But that would be deceitful double-dealing, sir. I wish you could make it another.	FESTE But that it would be double-dealing*, sir, I would you could make it another.

**Note: 'Double-dealing' – false dealing. Buying his friendship and a pun on wanting two coins.*

DUKE ORSINI Oh, you wish to make me guilty of double-dealing.	DUKE ORSINI O, you give me ill counsel.
FESTE Put your virtue in your pocket, sir, just this once, let your natural inclinations take over.	FESTE Put your grace in your pocket, sir, for this once, and let your flesh and blood obey it.
DUKE ORSINI Well, I'll make the small sin of being a double-dealer. Here's another then.	DUKE ORSINI Well, I will be so much a sinner to be a double-dealer. There's another.

ORSINI HANDS FESTE ANOTHER GOLD COIN.

FESTE First, second, third, is good game strategy, and the old saying goes, 'Third time lucky'. Triple time, sir, is a good dancing beat. Or the bells of Saint Bennet, sir, may remind you – (*Feste imitates church bells ringing*) one, two, three.	FESTE Primo, secundo, tertio, is a good play, and the old saying is `The third pays for all'; the triplex, sir, is a good tripping measure; or the bells of Saint Bennet, sir, may put you in mind - one, two, three.
DUKE ORSINI You can fool no more money out of me at this throw of the dice. If you will let your lady know I am here to speak with her, and bring her to me, it may awake my generosity further.	DUKE ORSINI You can fool no more money out of me at this throw. If you will let your lady know I am here to speak with her, and bring her along with you, it may awake my bounty further.
FESTE Then, sir, sing lullabies to your generosity till I return. I am going, sir, but I would not like you to think my desire of wanting more is the sin of greed. But, as you say, sir, let your generosity take a nap, I will awaken it shortly.	FESTE Marry, sir, lullaby to your bounty till I come again. I go, sir, but I would not have you to think that my desire of having is the sin of covetousness. But, as you say, sir, let your bounty take a nap; I will awake it anon.

EXIT FESTE.
ENTER ANTONIO AND OFFICERS, JOINING ORSINO, VIOLA, CURIO AND LORDS.

VIOLA (AS CESARIO)

Sir, here comes the man who rescued me.

VIOLA

Here comes the man, sir, that did rescue me.

DUKE ORSINI

I remember his face well. Yet when I last saw it, it was smeared as black as Vulcan by the gunpowder smoke of battle. He was captain of an insignificant vessel of shallow draught and little value, but with which he made such a destructive fight that he sunk the flagship of our fleet. Even those who suffered loss at his hands praised him with fame and honour. What's his offence?

DUKE ORSINI

That face of his I do remember well;
Yet when I saw it last it was besmeared
As black as Vulcan* in the smoke of war.
A baubling vessel was he captain of,
For shallow draught and bulk unprizable,
With which such scathful grapple did he make
With the most noble bottom of our fleet
That very envy and the tongue of loss
Cried fame and honour on him. What's the matter?

**Note: 'Vulcan' – Roman god of fire. Volcanoes are named after him.*

1ST OFFICER

Orsino, this is the same Antonio who captured the Phoenix and her cargo from Crete. And this is the man who boarded the Tiger which resulted in your young nephew Titus losing his leg. We found him in the street involved in a private quarrel with no regard for his shameful circumstances, and we apprehended him.

1ST OFFICER

Orsino, this is that Antonio
That took the Phoenix and her fraught from Candy;
And this is he that did the Tiger board
When your young nephew Titus lost his leg.
Here in the streets, desperate of shame and state,
In private brabble did we apprehend him.

VIOLA (AS CESARIO)

He did me a kindness, sir, he drew his sword to defend me. But afterwards he said some strange things to me. It made no sense, I thought it was some kind of madness.

VIOLA

He did me kindness, sir, drew on my side;
But in conclusion put strange speech upon me.
I know not what 'twas but distraction.

DUKE ORSINI

You notorious pirate, you salt-water thief, what foolish bravado brought you to the mercy of those whom in the most bloody and costly manner you have made your enemy?

DUKE ORSINI

Notable pirate, thou salt-water thief,
What foolish boldness brought thee to their mercies
Whom thou in terms so bloody and so dear
Hast made thine enemies?

ANTONIO

Orsino, noble sir, allow me to refute these names you give me. Antonio has never been a thief or a pirate, though I confess there are other grounds for me to be called Orsino's enemy. A bewitchment brought me here.

ANTONIO

Orsino, noble sir,
Be pleased that I shake off these names you give me.
Antonio never yet was thief or pirate,
Though I confess, on base and ground enough,
Orsino's enemy. A witchcraft drew me hither.

ANTONIO POINTS AT VIOLA (AS CESARIO).

ANTONIO (CONT'D)

I rescued that ungrateful boy there by your side from the cruel sea's angry and foamy mouth. If not for me there would have been no hope for him. I saved his life, and afterwards pledged my service to him unreservedly, I wholly dedicated myself to him. It was for his sake, and out of love for him that I exposed myself to the perils of this hostile town. I drew my sword to defend him when he had been beset upon, and after I was apprehended, he showed his deceit by not aiding me in my peril, telling me to my face he did not know me, and in one blink of the eye he turned into someone who had not known me for twenty years. And he denied he had my purse, which I had given to him for his own use not half an hour before.

ANTONIO

That most ingrateful boy there by your side
From the rude sea's enraged and foamy mouth
Did I redeem -a wrack past hope he was.
His life I gave him, and did thereto add
My love without retention or restraint,
All his in dedication. For his sake
Did I expose myself -pure for his love -
Into the danger of this adverse town;
Drew to defend him when he was beset;
Where being apprehended, his false cunning,
Not meaning to partake with me in danger,
Taught him to face me out of his acquaintance,
And grew a twenty years' removed thing
While one would wink; denied me mine own purse,
Which I had recommended to his use
Not half an hour before.

VIOLA (AS CESARIO)

(*disbelief*) How can this be?

VIOLA

How can this be?

DUKE ORSINI

When did he arrive in this town?

DUKE ORSINI

When came he to this town?

ANTONIO

Today, my lord, and for the past three months we've been together without a moment apart, both day and night.

ANTONIO

Today, my lord; and for three months before,
No int'rim, not a minute's vacancy,
Both day and night did we keep company.

ENTER OLIVIA WITH ATTENDANTS.

DUKE ORSINI

Here comes the countess. Heaven walking on earth!
(*to Antonio*) As for you, fellow – fellow, your words are madness. The last three months this youth has served me. But more of that later.
(*to Officers*) Take the man aside.

DUKE ORSINI

Here comes the countess. Now heaven walks on earth.
But for thee, fellow - fellow, thy words are madness.
Three months this youth hath tended upon me;
But more of that anon. Take him aside.

OLIVIA

(*to Orsini*) What does his lordship desire, except for that which he cannot have, that I, Olivia, may possibly be able to serve him with?
(*to Viola*) Cesario, you did not keep your promise to me.

OLIVIA

What would my lord, but that he may not have,
Wherein Olivia may seem serviceable?
Cesario, you do not keep promise with me.

VIOLA (AS CESARIO)

Madam?

VIOLA

Madam?

DUKE ORSINI Gracious Olivia…	DUKE ORSINI Gracious Olivia -
OLIVIA (*ignoring Orsini*) What have you to say for yourself, Cesario?	OLIVIA What do you say, Cesario?

ORSINI TRIES TO SAY SOMETHING, OLIVIA STOPS HIM.

OLIVIA (*to Orsini*) Wait my lord…	OLIVIA Good my lord -
VIOLA (AS CESARIO) My lord wishes to speak, my duty silences me.	VIOLA My lord would speak, my duty hushes me.
OLIVIA (*to Orsini*) If it's anything to do with the old tune you've been singing, my lord, it's as loud and distasteful to my ear as howling is to music.	OLIVIA If it be aught to the old tune, my lord, It is as fat and fulsome to mine ear As howling after music.
DUKE ORSINI Still so cruel?	DUKE ORSINI Still so cruel?
OLIVIA Still the same, my lord.	OLIVIA Still so constant, lord.
DUKE ORSINI The same stubbornness? You cruel lady, one to whose ungrateful and unwelcoming altars my soul has breathed out the truest vows of devotion that were ever uttered. What else can I do?	DUKE ORSINI What, to perverseness? You uncivil lady, To whose ingrate and unauspicious altars My soul the faithfull'st off'rings hath breathed out That e'er devotion tendered. What shall I do?
OLIVIA Whatever it is that pleases you, my lord, providing it is honourable.	OLIVIA Even what it please my lord that shall become him.
DUKE ORSINI If I had the heart to do it, why shouldn't I kill that which I love, like the Egyptian thief when he was at the point of death? – Savage jealousy in certain circumstances has an air of nobility.	DUKE ORSINI Why should I not, had I the heart to do it, Like to th' Egyptian thief* at point of death, Kill what I love? - a savage jealousy That sometime savours nobly.

**Note: 'Egyptian thief' – from the story of Theagenes and Chariclea in the Ethiopica of Heliodorus. The Egyptian thief, Thyamis, fell desperately in love with Chariclea, a lady he'd stolen from his enemy . After being overrun by a stronger band of thieves, he had her shut in a cave with his treasure. When he realised he was to be put to death he decided that no one else should marry Chariclea and she should join him in the afterlife. He entered the cave and in the darkness called out to her. Upon being answered by a voice he took to be hers, he plunged his dagger into the heart of the person. (it turns out it wasn't Chariclea).*

DUKE ORSINI (CONT'D)	DUKE ORSINI
But hear me out, since you cast my affections aside, and since I suspect I know what ousts me from my true place in your favour, then carry on living like a cold-hearted tyrant. But him…	But hear me this: Since you to non-regardance cast my faith, And that I partly know the instrument That screws me from my true place in your favour, Live you the marble-breasted tyrant still; But this...

ORSINI INDICATES VIOLA (AS CESARIO)

DUKE ORSINI (CONT'D)	DUKE ORSINI
…your darling, whom I know you love, and who by heaven I swear I regard dearly, I will tear him away from that cruel eye of yours where he sits crowned to spite his master.	...your minion, whom I know you love, And whom, by heaven, I swear I tender dearly, Him will I tear out of that cruel eye Where he sits crowned in his master's spite.

DUKE ORSINI TAKES A HOLD OFF VIOLA (AS CESARIO)

DUKE ORSINI (CONT'D)	DUKE ORSINI
Come with me, boy. My thoughts turn to revenge. *I'll sacrifice the lamb that I do love* *To spite a raven's heart within a dove.*	Come, boy, with me. My thoughts are ripe in mischief: *I'll sacrifice the lamb that I do love* *To spite a raven's heart within a dove.*
VIOLA (AS CESARIO)	VIOLA
And I, most willingly with happy sigh, *To bring you peace, a thousand deaths would die.*	*And I, most jocund, apt, and willingly,* *To do you rest, a thousand deaths would die.*

ORSINI MAKES TO LEAVE AND VIOLA (AS CESARIO) FOLLOWS.

OLIVIA	OLIVIA
Where's Cesario going?	Where goes Cesario?
VIOLA (AS CESARIO)	VIOLA
With the man I love. *More than I love my eyes, more than my life,* *More by far than ever I'll love a wife.* *And if I lie, let powers up above* *Take my life for dishonouring my love!*	After him I love *More than I love these eyes, more than my life,* *More, by all mores, than e'er I shall love wife.* *If I do feign, you witnesses above* *Punish my life for tainting of my love!*
OLIVIA	OLIVIA
Alas, I am despised. How I've been misled!	Ay me detested, how am I beguiled!
VIOLA (AS CESARIO)	VIOLA
Who does mislead you? Who has done you wrong?	*Who does beguile you? Who does do you wrong?*

OLIVIA
Have you forgot so fast, is it so long?
Go call the holy father.

OLIVIA
Hast thou forgot thyself? Is it so long?
Call forth the holy father.

EXIT ATTENDANT. ORSINI PULLS VIOLA AWAY BY THE ARM.

DUKE ORSINI
(to Viola) *Come away.*

DUKE ORSINI
[*To Viola.*] *Come, away.*

OLIVIA PULLS VIOLA BACK BY THE OTHER ARM.

OLIVIA
Where to, my lord? Cesario, husband, stay.

DUKE ORSINI
Husband?

OLIVIA
Yes, husband, can he that deny?

DUKE ORSINI
(to Viola) Her husband, young sir?

VIOLA (AS CESARIO)
No, my lord, not I.

OLIVIA
Alas, it is because of your fear of Orsino that you deny your position. Don't be afraid, Cesario, take possession of your fortunes, be who you know you really are, then you'll be as great as the one you fear.

OLIVIA
Whither, my lord? Cesario, husband, stay.

DUKE ORSINI
Husband?

OLIVIA
Ay, husband. Can he that deny?

DUKE ORSINI
Her husband, sirrah?

VIOLA
No, my lord, not I.

OLIVIA
Alas, it is the baseness of thy fear
That makes thee strangle thy propriety.
Fear not, Cesario, take thy fortunes up;
Be that thou know'st thou art, and then thou art
As great as that thou fear'st.

ENTER THE PRIEST.

OLIVIA (CONT'D)
Oh, welcome father! Father I ask you, as a holy man, to reveal – even though we had agreed to keep the occasion secret until the time was right - what you know has recently occurred between this youth and me.

OLIVIA
O welcome, father!
Father, I charge thee, by thy reverence,
Here to unfold - though lately we intended
To keep in darkness what occasion now
Reveals before 'tis ripe - what thou dost know
Hath newly passed between this youth and me.

PRIEST
A solemn vow of eternal love confirmed by the mutual joining of your hands, sealed with a holy kiss, strengthened by the exchange of your rings, confirmed in a ceremony before me, and blessed in my holy capacity and by my solemn oath, since when – as my watch tells me – only two hours of travel time towards my grave has passed.

PRIEST
A contract of eternal bond of love
Confirmed by mutual joinder of your hands,
Attested by the holy close of lips,
Strengthened by interchangement of your rings,
And all the ceremony of this compact
Sealed in my function, by my testimony;
Since when, my watch hath told me, toward my grave
I have travelled but two hours.

DUKE ORSINI
(*to Viola*) Oh, you deceitful fox cub! What will you be like when time has sprinkled grey on your hair?
Or will your cunning be so quickly grown
That by your own hands you'll be overthrown?
Farewell, and take her, but make sure your feet
Are never somewhere you and I may meet.

DUKE ORSINI
O thou dissembling cub! What wilt thou be
When time hath sowed a grizzle on thy case?
Or will not else thy craft so quickly grow
That thine own trip shall be thine overthrow?
Farewell, and take her; but direct thy feet
Where thou and I henceforth may never meet.

VIOLA (AS CESARIO)
My lord, I swear…

VIOLA
My lord, I do protest.*

**Note: 'Protest' then meant to swear an oath.*

OLIVIA
(*interrupting*) Oh, do not swear an oath. Keep a little back for me, even though you are frightened to.

OLIVIA
O, do not swear:
Hold little faith, though thou hast too much fear.

ENTER SIR ANDREW BLEEDING FROM THE HEAD.

SIR ANDREW AGUECHEEK
For the love of God, get a surgeon! And send one to Sir Toby too.

SIR ANDREW AGUECHEEK
For the love of God, a surgeon! Send one presently to Sir Toby.

OLIVIA
What has happened?

OLIVIA
What's the matter?

SIR ANDREW AGUECHEEK
He's broken my head, and given Sir Toby a bloody nose too. For the love of God, please help! I'd give forty pounds to be back at home.

SIR ANDREW AGUECHEEK
H'as broke my head across, and has given Sir Toby a bloody coxcomb* too. For the love of God, your help! I had rather than forty pound I were at home.

**Note: 'Coxcomb' – head, based on the fools cap.*

OLIVIA
Who has done this, Sir Andrew?

OLIVIA
Who has done this, Sir Andrew?

SIR ANDREW AGUECHEEK
The count's gentleman, Cesario. We thought he was a coward, but he's the devil incarnate!

DUKE ORSINI
My man, the gentleman Cesario?

SIR ANDREW AGUECHEEK
(*seeing Viola*) By God, he's here!
(*to Viola)* You broke my head for no reason, and what I did, I was made to do by Sir Toby.

VIOLA (AS CESARIO)
Why do you speak this way to me? I never hurt you. You drew your sword on me without reason, and I was courteous with you and didn't hurt you.

SIR ANDREW AGUECHEEK
If a bloody head is a hurt, then you have hurt me. I think you think nothing of a bloody head.

SIR ANDREW AGUECHEEK
The count's gentleman, one Cesario. We took him for a coward, but he's the very devil incardinate.

DUKE ORSINI
My gentleman Cesario?

SIR ANDREW AGUECHEEK
Od's-lifelings, here he is! You broke my head for nothing; and that that I did, I was set on to do't by Sir Toby.

VIOLA
Why do you speak to me? I never hurt you.
You drew your sword upon me without cause,
But I bespake you fair and hurt you not.

SIR ANDREW AGUECHEEK
If a bloody coxcomb be a hurt, you have hurt me. I think you set nothing by a bloody coxcomb.

ENTER A DRUNK, BLOODY FACED SIR TOBY, SUPPORTED BY FESTE.

SIR ANDREW AGUECHEEK (CONT'D)
Here comes Sir Toby, staggering, you'll hear more from him. If he hadn't been so drunk he would have beaten you properly.

DUKE ORSINI
What's happened, sir? What happened to you??

SIR TOBY BELCH
That's neither here nor there, he has hurt me, and there's nothing more to be said.
(*to Feste*) Fool, did you send for Dick Surgeon, fool?

SIR ANDREW AGUECHEEK
Here comes Sir Toby, halting; you shall hear more. But if he had not been in drink he would have tickled you othergates than he did.

DUKE ORSINI
How now, gentleman? How is't with you?

SIR TOBY BELCH
That's all one; h'as has hurt me, and there's th' end on't. Sot, didst see Dick Surgeon, sot?

**Note: 'Sot' – originally meant fool or foolish. It later changed to meaning drunkard.*

FESTE
Oh, Sir Toby, he's drunk an hour ago. His eyes went dark at eight this morning.

SIR TOBY BELCH
Then he's a rogue, always slow and staggering. I hate the drunken rogue. (*he staggers*)

FESTE
O, he's drunk, Sir Toby, an hour agone. His eyes were set at eight i'th' morning.

SIR TOBY BELCH
Then he's a rogue and a passy measures pavin. I hate the drunken rogue.

**Note: 'Passy measures pavin' – a slow dance, swaying side to side.*

OLIVIA (*to attendants*)Take him away! Who has caused this mayhem with them?	OLIVIA Away with him! Who hath made this havoc with them?
SIR ANDREW AGUECHEEK I'll help you, Sir Toby, we can be bandaged together.	SIR ANDREW AGUECHEEK I'll help you, Sir Toby, because we'll be dressed together.
SIR TOBY BELCH (*slurring*) You help? – you're an ass-head and an idiot, and a rogue, a thin faced rogue, a dolt.	SIR TOBY BELCH Will you help? - an ass-head and a coxcomb and a knave, a thin-faced knave, a gull.
OLIVIA Get him to bed, and let his wounds be looked at.	OLIVIA Get him to bed, and let his hurt be looked to.

EXEUNT FESTE, FABIAN, SIR TOBY, AND SIR ANDREW.
ENTER SEBASTIAN, WHO ADDRESSES HIS WIFE-TO-BE, OLIVIA.

SEBASTIAN (*to Olivia*) I'm sorry I injured your cousin, madam, but even if he had been my own brother I'd have done no less to ensure my safety. You look at me in a strange way, I think I have offended you. Pardon me, sweet lady, especially after the vows we made to each other so short a time ago..	SEBASTIAN I am sorry, madam, I have hurt your kinsman; But had it been the brother of my blood I must have done no less with wit and safety. You throw a strange regard upon me, and by that I do perceive it hath offended you. Pardon me, sweet one, even for the vows We made each other but so late ago.
DUKE ORSINI (*shocked surprise*) One face, one voice, one outfit, and two people. An optical illusion. Something that is, but isn't.	DUKE ORSINI One face, one voice, one habit, and two persons: A natural perspective, that is and is not.

SEBASTIAN SEES ANTONIO, WHO HE HAS BEEN SEARCHING FOR.

SEBASTIAN Antonio! Oh, my dear Antonio, how the hours have been torture to me since I lost touch with you!	SEBASTIAN Antonio, O my dear Antonio, How have the hours racked and tortured me Since I have lost thee!
ANTONIO Sebastian? Is it you?	ANTONIO Sebastian are you?
SEBASTIAN Do you doubt that, Antonio?	SEBASTIAN Fear'st thou that, Antonio?
ANTONIO How have you split yourself? An apple cut in two is not more alike than these two creatures. Which one is Sebastian?	ANTONIO How have you made division of yourself? An apple cleft in two is not more twin Than these two creatures. Which is Sebastian?

OLIVIA
This is incredible!

OLIVIA
Most wonderful!*

**Note: 'Wonderful' – then meant miraculous.*

ANTONIO POINTS OUT VIOLA WHO SEBASTIAN SEES FOR THE FIRST TIME.

SEBASTIAN STARES AT VIOLA IN DISBELIEF.

SEBASTIAN
(*stunned*) Is that me standing there? I never had a brother, nor do I have the divine gift of being in two places at once. I did have a sister, but she was devoured by the cruel sea.
(*to Viola*) Kindly tell me, are you related to me? What nationality, what name, what parentage?

SEBASTIAN
Do I stand there? I never had a brother;
Nor can there be that deity in my nature
Of here and everywhere. I had a sister,
Whom the blind waves and surges have devoured.
Of charity, what kin are you to me?
What countryman? What name? What parentage?

VIOLA (AS CESARIO)
From Messaline. Sebastian was my father, and Sebastian was my brother too. He was dressed as you are when he went to his watery tomb. If ghosts can assume both body and clothing then you have come to frighten us.

VIOLA
Of Messaline. Sebastian was my father;
Such a Sebastian was my brother too;
So went he suited to his watery tomb.
If spirits can assume both form and suit,
You come to fright us.

SEBASTIAN
I must be a ghost then, but in a dimension where I am clad as I was in the world from where I exited the womb. If you were a woman, which would make sense of everything, I would have tears falling down my cheeks and I'd say "Thrice welcome, drowned Viola!"

SEBASTIAN
A spirit I am indeed,
But am in that dimension grossly clad
Which from the womb I did participate.
Were you a woman, as the rest goes even,
I should my tears let fall upon your cheek
And say "Thrice welcome, drowned Viola!"*

**Note: 'Viola' – the first time her name is mentioned in the play.*

VIOLA (AS CESARIO)
My father had a mole on his forehead.

VIOLA
My father had a mole upon his brow.

SEBASTIAN
So did mine.

SEBASTIAN
And so had mine.

VIOLA (AS CESARIO)
And he died the day that Viola turned thirteen.

VIOLA
And died that day when Viola from her birth
Had numbered thirteen years.

SEBASTIAN
Oh, that memory is embedded into my soul. He did indeed end his mortal life the day my sister turned thirteen.

SEBASTIAN
O, that record is lively in my soul:
He finished indeed his mortal act
That day that made my sister thirteen years.

VIOLA (AS CESARIO)

If the only thing that hinders our happiness is these masculine clothes I've adopted, do not embrace me till every circumstance of place, time, and fortune, come together to conclusively prove I am Viola. And to confirm this I'll take you to a captain in this town who is looking after my female clothes, and by whose kind help I was saved to serve this noble count. All my life since then has been dedicated to this lady and this master.

VIOLA

If nothing lets to make us happy both
But this my masculine usurped attire,
Do not embrace me till each circumstance
Of place, time, fortune, do cohere and jump
That I am Viola; which to confirm
I'll bring you to a captain in this town,
Where lie my maiden weeds, by whose gentle help
I was preserved to serve this noble count.
All the occurrence of my fortune since
Hath been between this lady and this lord.

SEBASTIAN

(*to Olivia*) So that, lady, is how you were mistaken. Nature in her bias decided that you would have been married to a woman, but, upon my life, you were not deceived. You are now betrothed to both a woman *and* a man.

SEBASTIAN

[*To Olivia.*] So comes it, lady, you have been mistook;
But nature to her bias drew in that.
You would have been contracted to a maid;
Nor are you therein, by my life, deceived:
You are betrothed both to a maid and man.

DUKE ORSINI

Don't be alarmed, he is of noble blood. If this is true, as the mirror image seems to confirm, I'll have a share of this most happy salvage too.
(*to Viola*) My boy, you have said to me a thousand times that you'd never love a woman as much as you love me.

DUKE ORSINI

Be not amazed; right noble is his blood.
If this be so, as yet the glass seems true,
I shall have share in this most happy wrack.
[To Viola.] Boy, thou hast said to me a thousand times
Thou never shouldst love woman like to me.

VIOLA (AS HERSELF)

And all those sayings I'll swear again, and all those vows are as true in my heart as the sun is as true to each day.

VIOLA

And all those sayings will I overswear,
And all those swearings keep as true in soul
As doth that orbed continent the fire
That severs day from night.

DUKE ORSINI

Give me your hand, and let me see you in your own womanly clothes.

DUKE ORSINI

Give me thy hand;
And let me see thee in thy woman's weeds.

VIOLA

The captain who brought me to shore has my womanly clothes. He's under arrest for some legal action brought against him by Malvolio, a gentleman and servant of my lady's.

VIOLA

The captain that did bring me first on shore
Hath my maid's garments. He upon some action
Is now in durance, at Malvolio's suit,
A gentleman and follower of my lady's.

OLIVIA

He shall free him. Fetch Malvolio here. But wait, now I remember, they say the poor gentleman is not himself.

OLIVIA

He shall enlarge him. Fetch Malvolio hither.
And yet, alas, now I remember me,
They say, poor gentleman, he's much distract.

ENTER FESTE WITH A LETTER, AND FABIAN.

OLIVIA (CONT'D)
A madness of my own has made me forget his plight.
(*to Feste*) How is Malvolio, man?

FESTE
Truly, madam, he keeps the devil at bay as well as any man in his situation can. He's written a letter to you. I should have given it to you this morning, but as a madman's ramblings are not gospels, it is of no real matter when they are delivered.

OLIVIA
Open it and read it.

FESTE
Expect then to be educated on how a fool delivers the words of a madman.

OLIVIA
A most extracting frenzy of mine own
From my remembrance clearly banished his.
How does he, sirrah?

FESTE
Truly, madam, he holds Belzebub at the stave's end as well as a man in his case may do. H'as here writ a letter to you. I should have given't you today morning; but as a madman's epistles are no gospels, so it skills not much when they are delivered.

OLIVIA
Open't, and read it.

FESTE
Look then to be well edified when the fool delivers the madman.

FESTE READS, AS IF HE WERE A MADMAN.

FESTE
(*madly*) "By the Lord, madam…"

OLIVIA
(*stopping him*) What's this, are you mad now?

FESTE
No, madam, I am only reading madness. And your ladyship will have it read as it ought to be, you must excuse my impression.

OLIVIA
Please read it as yourself.

FESTE
That I will, madam, but to read it myself as him is to read it this way;
(*dramatically*) Therefore take heed, my princess, and lend me your ear.

OLIVIA
(*to Fabian*) You read it, Fabian.

FESTE
[*Reads madly.*]"By the Lord, madam," -

OLIVIA
How now, art thou mad?

FESTE
No, madam, I do but read madness. And your ladyship will have it as it ought to be, you must allow vox.

OLIVIA
Prithee read i'thy right wits.

FESTE
So I do, madonna; but to read his right wits is to read thus; therefore perpend, my princess, and give ear.

OLIVIA
[*To Fabian.*] Read it you, sirrah.

FABIAN TAKES THE LETTER FROM FESTE.

FABIAN
(*reads*) *"By the lord, madam, you do me wrong, and the world shall hear of it. Though you have locked me away in darkness, and put your drunken cousin in charge over me, still my senses are as sane as your ladyship's. I have your own letter which induced me to put on the act that I did, which will prove beyond doubt that I was in the right and it will also put you to much shame. Think of me as you please. I speak out of turn, but I speak out as one injured.*

The Madly-Used MALVOLIO."

OLIVIA
Did he write this?

FESTE
Yes, madam.

DUKE ORSINI
This doesn't sound much like madness.

OLIVIA
Set him free, Fabian, and bring him here.

FABIAN
[Reads.] "By the Lord, madam, you wrong me, and the world shall know it. Though you have put me into darkness, and given your drunken cousin rule over me, yet have I the benefit of my senses as well as your ladyship. I have your own letter that induced me to the semblance I put on; with the which I doubt not but to do myself much right, or you much shame. Think of me as you please. I leave my duty a little unthought of, and speak out of my injury.

THE MADLY-USED MALVOLIO."

OLIVIA
Did he write this?

FESTE
Ay, madam.

DUKE ORSINI
This savours not much of distraction.

OLIVIA
See him delivered, Fabian; bring him hither.

EXIT FABIAN.

OLIVIA (CONT'D)
(*to Orsini*) My lord, if it pleases you, when you've given further thought on the matter, I hope you'll accept me as a sister-in-law, rather than a wife, and if you'll agree, we can cement the alliances on the same day, at my house and at my expense.

DUKE ORSINI
Madam, I most readily accept your offer.
(*to Viola*) Your master releases you, and for the service you have done for him, against the nature of your sex, and far beneath the level of your soft and tender breeding, and since you have called me master for so long, here is my hand. You shall from this moment be your master's mistress.

OLIVIA
A sister! – That's who you are.

OLIVIA
My lord, so please you, these things further thought on,
To think me as well a sister as a wife,
One day shall crown th' alliance on't, so please you,
Here at my house and at my proper cost.

DUKE ORSINI
Madam, I am most apt t'embrace your offer.
[To Viola.] Your master quits you; and for your service done him,
So much against the mettle of your sex,
So far beneath your soft and tender breeding,
And since you called me master for so long,
Here is my hand; you shall from this time be
Your master's mistress.

OLIVIA
A sister! - you are she.

RE-ENTER FABIAN AND MALVOLIO.

DUKE ORSINI
Is this the madman?

OLIVIA
Yes, my lord, that is him.
(*to Malvolio*) How are you, Malvolio?

MALVOLIO
Madam, you have wronged me. A monstrous wrong.

OLIVIA
Have I, Malvolio? No.

MALVOLIO
Lady, you have. I ask you to read this letter. You cannot deny it is your handwriting.

DUKE ORSINI
Is this the madman?

OLIVIA
Ay, my lord, this same.
How now, Malvolio?

MALVOLIO
Madam, you have done me wrong,
Notorious wrong.

OLIVIA
Have I, Malvolio? No.

MALVOLIO
Lady, you have. Pray you peruse that letter.
You must not now deny it is your hand.

MALVOLIO PRODUCES THE LETTER HE FOUND AND HANDS IT TO OLIVIA.

MALVOLIO (CONT'D)
Try writing differently if you can, in handwriting or phrasing, or say this is not your seal, not your composition, you can't say it is not. Well, admit it then, and tell me on your honour why you have given me such clear signals of your favour, asked me to smile to you in cross-gartered yellow tights, and to talk down to Sir Toby and your staff. And after carrying all this out in obedient hope, why did you have me imprisoned, kept in a dark room, visited by a priest, and made the biggest fool out of me that was ever fooled. Tell me why?

MALVOLIO
Write from it, if you can, in hand or phrase,
Or say 'tis not your seal, not your invention.
You can say none of this. Well, grant it then,
And tell me, in the modesty of honour,
Why you have given me such clear lights of favour,
Bade me come smiling and cross-gartered to you,
To put on yellow stockings, and to frown
Upon Sir Toby and the lighter people;
And, acting this in an obedient hope,
Why have you suffered me to be imprisoned,
Kept in a dark house, visited by the priest,
And made the most notorious geck and gull
That e'er invention played on? Tell me why?

OLIVIA
I'm sorry, Malvolio, this is not my writing. Though I confess it is very similar. Without a doubt it is Maria's handwriting. And now I think about it, it was she who first told me you were mad. Then you came in smiling, and following the instructions you were given in the letter. So be assured, this joke has been most shrewdly played on you, and when we know the reasons and the people behind it you shall be both judge and jury for your own case.

OLIVIA
Alas, Malvolio, this is not my writing,
Though I confess much like the character;
But out of question 'tis Maria's hand.
And now I do bethink me, it was she
First told me thou wast mad; then cam'st in smiling,
And in such forms which here were presupposed
Upon thee in the letter. Prithee be content.
This practice hath most shrewdly passed upon thee;
But when we know the grounds and authors of it,
Thou shalt be both the plaintiff and the judge
Of thine own cause.

FABIAN

Good madam, let me speak, to prevent a dispute or brawl arising to spoil this moment, which has greatly amazed me. In the hope it does, I most freely confess that myself and Toby set up this prank against Malvolio here, because of some stubborn and discourteous behaviour of his we had taken exception to. Maria wrote the letter, under Sir Toby's instruction, and as compensation for it he has since married her.

FABIAN

Good madam, hear me speak,
And let no quarrel nor no brawl to come
Taint the condition of this present hour,
Which I have wondered at. In hope it shall not,
Most freely I confess myself and Toby
Set this device against Malvolio here,
Upon some stubborn and uncourteous parts
We had conceived against him. Maria writ
The letter, at Sir Toby's great importance,
In recompense whereof he hath married her.

GASPS OF SURPRISE FROM THOSE GATHERED.

FABIAN (CONT'D)

How the playful malice was carried out may induce laughter rather than warrant revenge, if the injuries on all parties are weighed up.

FABIAN

How with a sportful malice it was followed
May rather pluck on laughter than revenge,
If that the injuries be justly weighed
That have on both sides passed.

OLIVIA

(*to Malvolio*) Alas, poor fool, how they have made a fool of you!

OLIVIA

[To Malvolio.] Alas, poor fool, how have they baffled thee!

FESTE

Yes, "*some are born great, some achieve greatness, and some have greatness thrust upon them*". I played a part in this production sir, I was Sir Topas, sir, but that's not important.
(*imitating Malvolio*) "*By the Lord, fool, I am not mad*!" And do you remember saying, "*Madam, why laugh at such an empty headed fool, Unless you laugh and pander to him he is silenced.*" And so the whirligig of time brings about revenge.

FESTE

Why, "some are born great, some achieve greatness, and some have greatness thrown upon them". I was one, sir, in this interlude, one Sir Topas, sir; but that's all one. "By the Lord, fool, I am not mad." But do you remember, "Madam, why laugh you at such a barren rascal. And you smile not, he's gagged"? And thus the whirligig of time brings in his revenges.

MALVOLIO

I'll get revenge on the whole lot of you!

MALVOLIO

I'll be revenged on the whole pack of you.

MALVOLIO STORMS OUT.

OLIVIA

He has been most outrageously abused.

OLIVIA

He hath been most notoriously abused.

DUKE ORSINI
(*to Fabian*) Go after him, and make peace with him. He hasn't told us about the captain yet. When that is sorted out, and at a golden moment, a solemn joining of our dear souls shall be made.
(*to Olivia*) In the meantime, sweet sister, we will wait here.
(*to Viola*) Come with me, Cesario, for that's how you'll be known while you're a man.
Till when in other outfits you are seen,
As Orsino's mistress, and his dear queen.

DUKE ORSINI
Pursue him, and entreat him to a peace;
He hath not told us of the captain yet.
When that is known, and golden time convents,
A solemn combination shall be made
Of our dear souls. Meantime, sweet sister,
We will not part from hence. Cesario, come;
For so you shall be while you are a man;
But when in other habits you are seen,
Orsino's mistress, and his fancy's queen.

EXEUNT ALL EXCEPT FESTE WHO SINGS A SONG.

FESTE
(sing) Back when I was a little tiny boy,
With a hey-ho, the wind and the rain,
My foolishness was just a toy,
For the rain it rains down every day.

But when I came to man's estate,
With a hey-ho, the wind and the rain,
'Gainst rogues like me men shut their gate,
For the rain it rains down every day.

But when I came, alas, to wed,
With a hey-ho, the wind and the rain,
My fooling couldn't keep us fed,
For the rain it rains down every day.

But when I came to go to bed,
With a hey-ho, the wind and the rain,
With drunkards I would lay my head,
For the rain it rains down every day.

A great while ago the world begun,
With a hey-ho, the wind and the rain,
But enough of that, our play is done,
And we'll strive to please you every day.

FESTE
[Sings.] When that I was and a little tiny boy,
With hey, ho, the wind and the rain,
A foolish thing was but a toy,
For the rain it raineth every day.

But when I came to man's estate,
With hey, ho, the wind and the rain,
'Gainst knaves and thieves men shut their gate,
For the rain it raineth every day.

But when I came, alas, to wive,
With hey, ho, the wind and the rain,
By swaggering could I never thrive,
For the rain it raineth every day.

But when I came unto my beds,
With hey, ho, the wind and the rain,
With tosspots still had drunken heads,
For the rain it raineth every day.

A great while ago the world begun,
With hey, ho, the wind and the rain,
But that's all one, our play is done,
And we'll strive to please you every day.

THE END

Printed in Great Britain
by Amazon